Happy Handmaking
Katie
xo Blair Chu

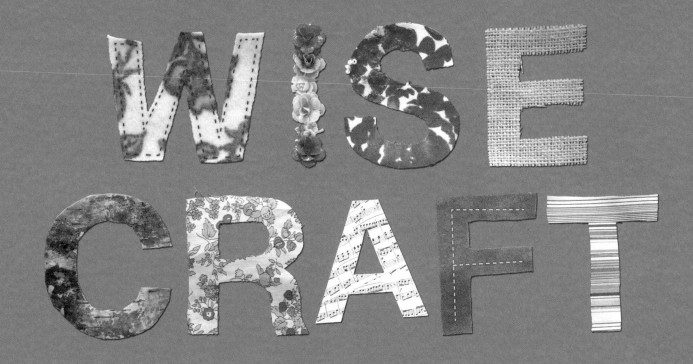

WISE CRAFT

Turning Thrift Store Finds, Fabric Scraps, and
Natural Objects into Stuff You Love

BLAIR STOCKER

RUNNING PRESS
PHILADELPHIA · LONDON

Books published by Running Press are available at special discounts for bulk purchases
in the United States by corporations, institutions, and other organizations.
For more information, please contact the Special Markets Department at the Perseus Books Group,
2300 Chestnut Street, Suite 200, Philadelphia, PA 19103, or call (800) 810-4145, ext. 5000, or
e-mail special.markets@perseusbooks.com.

ISBN 978-0-7624-4969-9
Library of Congress Control Number: 2013943532
E-book ISBN 978-0-7624-5183-8

9 8 7 6 5 4 3 2 1
Digit on the right indicates the number of this printing

Cover and interior design by Susan Van Horn
Illustrations by Lisa Congdon
Edited by Kristen Green Wiewora
Typography: Mr. Eaves, Matchmaker, Gotham, and Rockford

Running Press Book Publishers
2300 Chestnut Street
Philadelphia, PA 19103–4371

Visit us on the web!
www.runningpress.com

To Peter, Emma, and Ian, who taught me
how a house can be a home.

And to "Mom" Fletcher, who taught me
how to make it homemade.

CONTENTS

ACKNOWLEDGMENTS

EJ Armstrong: Thank you for a truly wonderful collaboration. All those days playing around with ideas in your studio, and look at this! Your photography expertise and advice are invaluable!

Lisa Congdon: Your beautiful illustrations brought a new level of inspiration to these projects. Thank you, friend.

Peter, Emma, and Ian: "Thank you" will never be enough. You make me want to be better at everything I do, and always give me the best kind of advice (and the best hugs).

Jennifer: You truly are the best friend a girl could have. Thank you for always, *always* making the time to give advice and guidance.

Kristen and everyone at Running Press: Thank you for your expert guidance and belief in what this book could be.

Lisa Solomon: Thank you for taking valuable time from your own work to pattern test for me. You are wonderful.

Yi-Lin Lui: Thank you for providing your talent for the Gathering Bag project.

To friends who have been there for advice, guidance, and support for me as I was writing this book: Melissa Franz, Erin Harris, Christiane Zweifler, Amy Karol, Emily Demsky, Xiaonan Wang, and countless others. The support you all give means so much more than you know.

A huge, heartfelt thank you to the readers and supporters of *Wise Craft*. Thank you for being there, for making things with me, for being inspired by my corner of the world. This book would not be possible without you.

INTRODUCTION

A beloved old wool coat becomes a checkers set for the family. Outgrown or worn-through jeans are transformed into a beautiful and functional quilt. Branches gathered on a family walk become hooks to hold coats and bags. *Wise Craft* is about looking at your belongings with new eyes. It's about nurturing creativity by using less and appreciating more.

Throughout history, people have treasured handmade items. Even today, when many of our "valuables" are disposable and mass-produced, cookie-cutter material goods, there is a large segment of society that remains devoted to ancient ideals of handcrafting. There is an innate desire to create items by hand, to build a more personal connection to our possessions and surroundings. Combine this artistic sensibility with the modern awareness of repurposing and reusing, and you have *Wise Craft*.

I started my website Wise Craft in 2005 to share my story of handcrafting online. I never imagined it would inspire such a devoted and global following. Clearly, I am not alone in my passion for making unique, visually pleasing objects from existing materials. My goal is simply to make things that I like or can use and my inspiration almost always starts with something I've purchased secondhand or pulled from my closet or basement. I find that the process of creating something new from a tired or neglected item makes it feel more special, more intentional. I am not militantly "green" or obsessed with thrift. I just find that creating original pieces from gathered goods gives me a more personal connection to my surroundings and environment. It establishes a sense of value: of place, of family, of personal history.

I started handcrafting as a child, alongside my maternal grandmother. Under her guidance, I learned gardening, baking, knitting, and an appreciation for making things with my hands. I took to it immediately and felt a great sense of satisfaction discovering what I could create at a very early age. I rediscovered handcrafting when I became a mother. It has helped me connect with my kids and to nurture my own maternal role as keeper of family memories and traditions.

Never is my mind calmer than when I am sewing strips of fabric for a quilt, counting crochet stitches, or drawing in my sketchbook. Ideas, colors, patterns, and materials have become ways I express myself artistically. My kids are now old enough to appreciate the industry, creativity, beauty, and value of items in our home. And with each handmade addition to our household, I am bettering our surroundings, not just adding another cheap imported knickknack to the local landfill. Each stitch of what I make matters. It is part of our home, part of who I am, of who we are as a family. And there is something utterly satisfying knowing that the DNA of our home and lifestyle is not bought from a store shelf but meticulously stitched, snipped, and glued together by hand.

Because each season brings a sense of change and new inspiration for me creatively, there are four season-specific sections in this book, each with a distinctive color palette to draw inspiration from. Within each of these seasonal stories, there are a variety of projects, some doable in an afternoon or less, and some that require a little more time and thought. However, there is no need to confine the projects to the seasonal section they are in. The projects here are yours to adapt to any time of year, in any way that fits your own creative world. I hope you find inspiration from these projects and craft your own body of work, born from your own hands.

Enjoy,

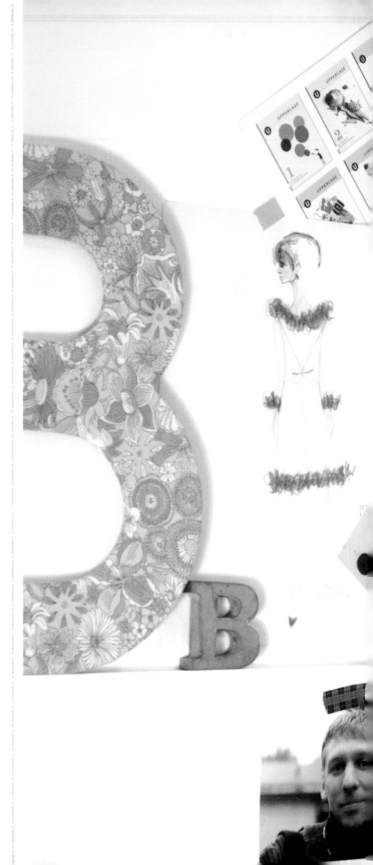

CRAFTER'S TOOLKIT

This book covers a wide variety of handcrafts, and it's much easier to jump right in when the inspiration strikes if you have a toolkit of basic supplies at the ready. Store the smaller items together in a basket or bin, and you'll be ready to go when the time and inclination hits.

1) All-purpose cleaner, cloths, and paper towels: Items purchased secondhand always need a good cleaning before you begin your project. (Plus, all good makers clean up their messes.)

2) A variety of pens and pencils: Ones I like to have on hand are mechanical pencils, fine-point and ultrafine-point black Sharpie pens, and water-soluble marking pens (whose marks disappear with a spritz of water). I most often use and recommend FriXion pens. Available at office supply stores, these pens write like a marker (and come in a variety of colors) but disappear with heat from an iron. Always test on a scrap first. I have heard that the marks made with these pens can come back when exposed to cold temperatures. I use these regularly and have never had that happen, and if it did, ironing could make the marks disappear once more.

3) Scissors: Designate ones for paper, for fabric, and all-purpose. Label them and hide them from the family.

4) A rotary cutter and a self-healing cutting mat: Generally used by quilters, these tools do double duty for cutting fabric or paper.

5) A craft knife with extra blades (also called a penknife or X-Acto knife).

6) A variety of tape, such as clear all-purpose tape, double-sided tape, painter's blue tape.

7) An iron and ironing board.

8) Straight and safety pins.

9) A yardstick, ruler, and tape measure, as well as at least one all-purpose quilter's clear ruler (a good size for multiple uses is 8 x 24 inches).

10) A variety of glues, such as Mod Podge, rubber cement, and a hot glue gun. Aleen's Super Fabric Adhesive is a great one to have for gluing anything to fabric.

11) A sewing machine in good working order, a variety of machine needles, and coordinating thread: No fancy machines are needed for these projects, but my advice is to always start with a fresh needle and good-quality all-purpose cotton or cotton/poly thread.

12) A variety of hand-sewing needles and a thimble: One of those variety packs from the fabric store would be fine, plus a variety pack of tapestry needles with larger eyes and size 9 crewel embroidery needles (for threading yarn or perle cotton) would be good to have.

13) Embroidery hoops: Pick up a variety of sizes inexpensively at craft or even thrift stores, to have on hand.

14) Acrylic paint: Keep a few basic colors on hand.

15) A variety of paintbrushes.

16) Items to protect you and your workspace: newspaper or a drop cloth (e.g., an old bedsheet), rubber gloves, a face mask, and an apron.

17) Screwdrivers: flat and Phillips head.

18) A hammer and small nails.

19) Sandpaper.

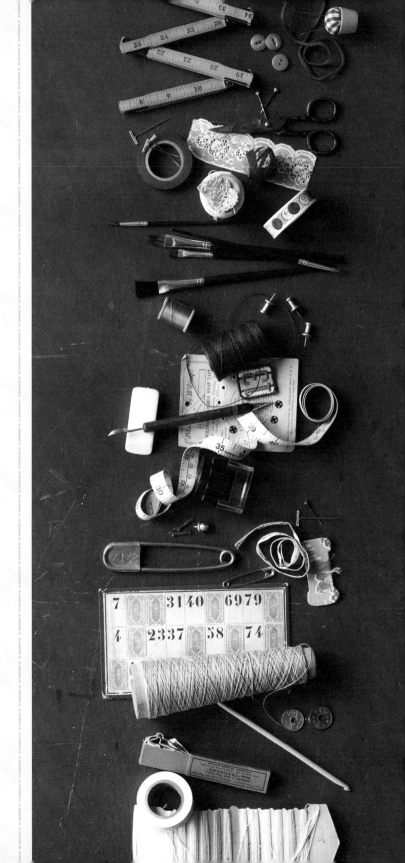

CHAPTER ONE

SPRING

*"Is the spring coming?" he said.
"What's it like?"
"It is the sun shining on the rain and
the rain falling on the sunshine..."*

—FRANCES HODGES BURNETT, *THE SECRET GARDEN*

mentally renewing, awake with the feeling of endless possibilities: I truly love spring. Nature stirs and perks up and so, it seems, do we. This is when I deep clean and freshen the house from top to bottom, tip to tail. It's the only time all year I seem to have the energy and motivation for this, so I go with it. Once that's done, I make things. A new quilt, some art for the walls, or maybe new pieces to set the dinner table with—whatever inspires me and feels right.

May Day Cones p.18

Leather Coasters p.21

Hot Plate Novels p.22

Art Book Wall p.25

Pot Handle Covers p.26

Covered Journals p.28

Statement Dishes p.31

Conversation Tablecloth p.32

Recycled Floral Mirror p.35

Leather-Covered Rocks p.37

Glittered Art p.41

Pebble & Beach Glass necklace p.42

Hand-loomed Placemats p.45

Crocheted Treasure Bag p.47

Pinpoint Oxford Eiderdown Coverlet p.51

May Day Cones

May Day cones are traditionally given on the first day of May as a celebration of spring. My kids and I have been known to leave them on neighbors' front doorknobs, ring the bell, then (the kids' favorite part) dash away. Commonly filled with fresh flowers, these versions are also filled with a small plant, providing something that can be enjoyed longer. Old sheet music and brown kraft paper are all that's needed to create a beautiful cone.

MATERIALS:

Brown kraft paper (e.g., a paper grocery bag)

Sheet music (I purchased mine at a thrift store)

Sandwich-size plastic bag

A small plant with roots (e.g., a fern, ivy, or succulent)

Flowers, stems cut to 5 to 6 inches long

Single hole punch

Scraps of ribbon about 18 inches long

From the Crafter's Toolkit:

Paper scissors

Double-sided tape

TO MAKE:

1) **Cut the kraft paper to size.** Cut the brown kraft paper to match the size of a single sheet of music.

2) **Make the cone.** With the plain side of the brown paper showing on the outside, fold it into a cone shape and secure with double-sided tape. Fold the sheet music into a cone shape and secure with double-sided tape. Slip the sheet music cone over the brown paper cone, leaving the edges of the brown paper visible at the top. Use double-sided tape to secure the cones together.

3) **Fill the cone.** Remove the plant from its container and fit the roots and soil inside the plastic sandwich bag. Slip this down securely inside the cone. Add the flowers by poking them into and around the plant.

4) **Create a hanger for the cone.** Punch two holes, 1 inch from the top edge, on opposite sides from each other at the top of the cone, through both layers of paper. Thread through a length of ribbon to hang with, and tie the ends.

OTHER IDEA:

* Instead of inserting plants and flowers, fill with crayons and rolled coloring pages and leave on the doorknob of a child's room.

Leather Coasters

When shopping secondhand, keep your eyes open for leather clothing: It can provide inexpensive leather for all kinds of projects. For these coasters, I traced silhouette images of my family and cut them out. Now, my kids think it's pretty funny to put drinks on our faces. The patina that develops through use gives them added charm and interesting imperfections, but you can spray them with a protector, such as Scotchgard, if you prefer, to help them hold up to water rings and drips.

MATERIALS:

Digital camera

Printer

All-purpose printer paper

A piece of leather at least 4 x 4 inches, for each coaster

From the Crafter's Toolkit:

Sharp scissors

FriXion pen or mechanical pencil

Craft glue (I used Mod Podge) (optional)

Paintbrush (optional)

TO MAKE:

1) **Create the silhouette images.** Take profile photos of your family's faces (don't forget the pets!). Adjust the size of each image to be at least 3½ x 3½ inches and print out onto all-purpose printer paper. Cut out the image, trying to keep in any interesting details (I kept my son's cowlick).

2) **Transfer the silhouettes to the leather.** Trace the silhouette shape onto the back of the leather, using a FriXion pen or a light pencil line. Cut out the silhouette.

   Optionally, use the leather silhouette alone as it is, or glue onto a slightly larger square of leather by applying craft glue to the back of the silhouette with a paintbrush.

OTHER IDEAS

* Use your sewing machine fitted with a leather or denim needle to add contrast stitching ¼ inch from the edge, all the way around, or stitch designs in the center of the coaster.

* Paint an allover design directly on the leather, using acrylic paint.

Hot Plate Novels

This simple idea creates a totally new use for books that end up on thrift store shelves. They can protect your table from hot pots and also look modern and elegant. I used hardcover books, because I prefer to remove the spine and cover completely. That's not as easy to do with paperback books. If there is a spill, simply rip off the top page and the hot plate is ready to be used for the next dinner gathering.

MATERIALS:

Hardcover books

From the Crafter's Toolkit:

Craft knife

Acrylic paint

Assorted paintbrushes

TO MAKE:

1) **Prepare the book.** Cut the cover off the book, using a craft knife. One clean cut close to the spine, inside the front and back covers, should remove the cover completely.

2) **Embellish the top page.** Paint a solid color, flowers, or other designs on the top page of the book. Another idea is to paint words over the pages. Let dry completely before using.

Art Book Wall

A step up from the Vogue covers I used to patchwork together on the walls of my bedroom when I was a teenager, this is a unique way to enjoy the pages of a beautiful book and hide walls that may not look their best. These pages were taken from a book found on eBay, but part of the fun is scouting used bookstores and thrift shops for the perfect book. We did a similar project in our kids' bathroom using pages from a Japanese graphic novel. Books with botanical illustrations or atlas pages would look great, too.

MATERIALS:

Book of your choice
(illustrations or photos work well)

Old credit card or putty knife

Thumbtacks or push pins

From the Crafter's Toolkit:

All-purpose cleaner and cloth

Newspaper or drop cloth to protect work surface

Craft knife

Craft glue (I used Mod Podge)

Paintbrushes

TO MAKE:

1) **Prepare the wall.** Clean the wall and allow it to dry.

2) **Cut out the book pages.** Lay down newspaper or a drop cloth, to protect your work surface. Cut out the book pages cleanly, using a craft knife. Prepare as many pages as you think you will use and play with placement before you start adhering the pages to the wall.

3) **Glue the pages to the wall.** Lay a page facedown on your protected work surface and completely cover the back of the page with craft glue, using a brush. Carefully place it on the wall and smooth out any wrinkles or bubbles with the edge of a credit card or putty knife. Do this with each page. Hang individual pages over these glued pages with thumbtacks for a dimensional effect.

Pot Handle Covers

I love unexpected homemade touches around the house, like these handle covers, and I always feel very clever and organized when I use them. We can all use a bit of that. They stitch up quickly and simply slip over hot handles to protect your hands when cooking.

MATERIALS:

Pots with oven-safe handles (e.g., cast-iron skillets)

Paper

Felted knits or leather scraps

Scrap pieces of quilt batting or Insul-Brite (I used both)

From the Crafter's Toolkit:

Pencil or pen

Paper and fabric scissors

Sewing machine and coordinating thread

Straight pins

TO MAKE:

1) **Prepare a paper template and cut out the pieces.** Using a pencil and paper, roughly trace around the pot's handle to create a template and cut it out (it will look like a big U). Using this template, cut two pieces of felted knits or leather scraps, and four pieces of quilt batting or Insul-Brite, each ½ inch larger than your traced template. When finished, a double layer of batting will line the handle cover all the way around.

2) **Prepare each side of the handle cover.** With the fabric right side up and two layers of batting underneath, machine stitch across the top of the U, where the opening for the handle will be, about ¼ inch from the edge. Repeat with other set of fabric and batting.

3) **Sew the handle together.** Pin the two layers together with their batting sides facing. Pin the paper template to the center, if desired, to use as a guide, then carefully stitch around the U shape, staying close to the outside edge.

4) **Trim the edges.** Clean up and trim around the edges, if needed.

Covered Journals

We are a family of doodlers, note takers, list makers, scribblers, and writers, and we each have our own favorite kind of journal to write in. My favorite is the classic Moleskine. The assortment of sizes and simple design works well for me. But because I can't leave things alone, I like to make the covers of these journals a little more personal. This is a quick and fun method I've used for years, to cover all kinds of journals. Test the opaqueness of the fabric you plan to use by holding it over the cover to see what shows through. Consider giving a set of these as a gift to friends and fellow doodlers.

MATERIALS:

Blank notebook(s) of your choice (paper or kraft paper covers allow you to add a button closure)

Double-sided fusible web for heavyweight fabric (I used Pellon Wonder Under)

Fabric to cover the outside of the journal (e.g., corduroy, denim, canvas, or home decor–weight)

Notions, for closures (e.g., buttons, strips of fabric or ribbon, leather, or elastic)

From the Crafter's Toolkit:

Iron and ironing board

Pencil

Fabric scissors

Paper scissors

Hand-sewing needle and coordinating thread

All-purpose glue

TO MAKE:

1) **Preheat your iron.** Following the package instructions on the fusible web, preheat your iron and have it ready.

2) **Prepare the fusible web.** Fully open the journal, laying it flat, pages facing up, over the fusible web. Using a pencil, trace around the journal onto the web. Cut out the web a bit larger than the traced outline.

3) **Adhere the fusible web to the fabric.** Lay the fabric right side down on the ironing board and press smooth. Lay the piece of fusible web over the fabric (glue side facing the fabric, paper side up) and, following the package instructions, iron over the fusible web to adhere it to the fabric. Allow to cool, then peel away the backing paper.

4) **Adhere the fabric to the journal cover.** Open the journal, cover side down, and place over the side of the fabric that has the fusible web. Be sure the journal fits completely inside the fusible web area *(see illustration)*. Close the journal, holding the fabric snugly around the outside of the journal. Iron the front side first, then flip the journal over and iron the back side (still keeping

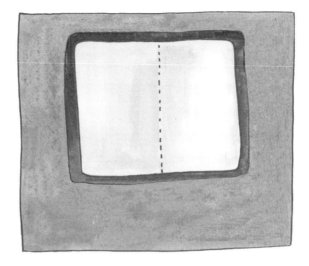

Position opened book, cover side down, within the fusible web area on the wrong side of the fabric.

the journal closed). Lastly, hold the iron over the spine area, to be sure the fabric is adhered there as well.

5) **Clean up the cover's edges.** Trim away any excess fabric around the journal, flush to the journal's edge (raw edges are totally okay here). Use the iron to touch up any areas that didn't adhere well the first time, especially around the journal's edges.

6) **Add a closure.** To add a button to a paper or kraft paper journal cover, sew a button right through the journal's front or back cover with a hand-sewing needle and thread. Glue the end of a length of ribbon to the journal cover, just under the button. To close the journal, wrap the ribbon a

couple of times around the journal, winding it around the button to secure. (Confession: My daughter's hair elastics work really well for me in a pinch for a hardcover journal.)

OTHER IDEAS:

* Add a pocket to the outside of the journal by using a cuff from an old sweater or pocket from a pair of jeans, sewn directly to the journal's paper cover.

* Use a belt loop cut from that same old pair of jeans and attach to the cover to create a pen holder.

Statement Dishes

None of our dishes match. Well, I guess they are all white (and usually chipped), so that's matching in a way. I played with a set of white dishes by putting generic words onto them, using a Pebeo Porcelaine 150 china marker. Doing this on all of them makes them a set, right? Try adding a favorite phrase to inspire you as you drink your morning coffee. Keep the lettering simple and in one color.

MATERIALS:

Assorted white dishes

Rubbing alcohol and cotton balls

A list of words, phrases, and inspirations to put on the dishes

Scrap paper (optional)

Computer (optional)

Printer (optional)

All-purpose printer paper (optional)

Pebeo Porcelaine 150 china marker in black or your choice of color

From the Crafter's Toolkit:

Pencil

Ruler (optional)

TO MAKE:

1) **Wash and dry all the dishes.** Give the area you'll write on a final wipe with a little alcohol on a cotton ball, to remove fingerprints.

2) **Create the design.** Practice writing out on scrap paper what you'll be adding to the dishes, or type into your computer, playing with sizing and placement, and print out. Don't make yourself crazy; aim for legible, neatly written lettering. A ruler is helpful to line everything up. Ideas could be Baby's first word, a favorite color, or even generic words, such as *pot* or *lid*. Perhaps channel Magritte, proclaiming, "This is not a plate!"

3) **Paint the dishes.** Once you're ready to write on the dishes, make things easier by lightly writing the phrase or word first in pencil (which will wash off later). Draw the outline of the letters first, then fill in with the marker. Slow down and enjoy this step. Music helps; a glass of wine helps more.

4) Allow the words to dry completely. Following the directions on the marker package, bake the pieces in the oven before using.

OTHER IDEA:

* Have your children draw directly onto the dishes with the markers. Simple line images are best.

Conversation Tablecloth

If you've ever seen a random group of kids (or adults) that don't know one another sitting together awkwardly at a dinner table, then you know what inspired this idea. My family and I came up with a list of conversation starters—"finish this sentence" examples, and "what ifs"—which I then transferred onto a plain white tablecloth, using a combination of embroidery and heat-transfer paper. Kids absolutely love this tablecloth. (Actually, adults do, too!) At your next dinner, consider leaving out a few fabric markers to let your guests add even more questions.

MATERIALS:

Computer

Printer

Printable heat-transfer sheets, appropriate for your home printer (I used Avery)

Light-colored cotton tablecloth or bedsheet

Embroidery thread (I used DMC)

From the Crafter's Toolkit:

Paper scissors

Straight pins

Iron and ironing board

FriXion pen or water-soluble fabric marker

Embroidery hoop

Embroidery needle

TO MAKE:

1) **Get some inspiration.** Brainstorm questions and "finish this sentence" examples with your family (or search online) and type them on your computer, playing with available fonts, sizes, and colors. Keep in mind you will want to fill each heat-transfer page with as much text as it can hold, to minimize waste, and that you may need to reverse the text (mirror image) before printing it out. Print out, following the package instructions.

2) **Place and adhere the transfers.** Cut out the words and questions, and play with placement on the top of the tablecloth before ironing them on. I purposely left the middle of the tablecloth a little cleaner and filled in the areas around the individual place settings and down the sides a little more densely. Pin the words to your tablecloth before moving it to the ironing board. Iron each phrase onto the front of the cloth, according to package directions.

3) **Write out words to embroider.** If you decide to embroider some of the questions as I did, sketch your words or design directly on the front of the tablecloth, using a FriXion pen or water-soluble marker. Using an embroidery hoop, needle, and your choice of embroidery thread, embroider the words, using a simple backstitch. To create a backstitch, first make a single stitch along the drawn line. Next, insert the needle up through the back, ¼ inch away from the first stitch, still following your line, then insert the needle back into the second hole of the previous stitch. Continue in this manner to stitch over all the letters and words.

OTHER IDEAS:

* Have guests sign their names on the tablecloth, then go back and embroider over the signatures.

* Illustrated riddles drawn with fabric markers are fun, too.

I hope tomorrow is

have you ever read...

If I were a color,
I would be ...

Earliest childhood
memory

I absolutely
refuse to ...

life is full of...

What would you do if you
were invisible for a day?

or O's
Tic Toc Toe?

Recycled Flower Mirror

Mirrors and their frames are easy to enhance and personalize. I made this floral mirror for my daughter Emma's room when we changed it from "little girl" to "big girl." The frame was purchased secondhand for under ten dollars, and the individual flowers were a cinch to make. They are very easy to throw in your bag for crafting on the go.

MATERIALS:

A sturdy wooden picture frame suitable for a mirror insert, or a preframed mirror

Spray paint

Scraps of felted sweaters, craft felt, quilting cottons, Ultrasuede, leather

Scraps of coordinating yarn (optional)

Picture-hanging hardware (optional)

Note: If you need a new mirror for the frame, it's best to have it cut and installed into the frame after you paint the frame, but before you add the flowers. Here's a little trick I've learned from mirror cutters. Before having the mirror installed, but after you've painted the frame, lay it on your newspaper-protected work surface with the back of the frame facing up. Using either a thick black marker or black paint and a small brush, blacken just the inside edge of the frame that the mirror will mount into. This small area will be reflected in the mirror and darkening it makes it visually disappear.

From the Crafter's Toolkit:

Newspaper or drop cloth to protect work surface

Painter's blue tape (optional)

All-purpose cleaner and cloth

Sandpaper

Face mask

Rubber gloves

Apron

Thick black Sharpie pen or black acrylic paint with a small brush (optional)

Fine-point pen or pencil

Ruler

Fabric scissors

Sewing machine and coordinating thread

Hand-sewing needle

Hot glue gun

TO MAKE:

1) **Prepare and paint the frame.** Lay down newspaper or a drop cloth to protect your work surface. Take any picture or old mirror out of the frame and discard, or tape off the mirror, using painter's blue tape. Clean the wood and give it a light sanding to prepare it for painting, wiping it thoroughly afterward. Don the face mask, rubber gloves, and apron. Give the front and back of the frame several thin coats of spray paint. Allow to dry completely.

2) **Create the flowers.** Using a pen and ruler, mark and cut your fabric into long strips (about 11 x 3 inches for the first few, but start to vary the width and length with each flower, to create a nice variety of sizes as you continue to make them).

Fold a strip in half length-wise and machine stitch the cut edges together down the length of the fabric strip, using a ¼-inch seam allowance. Next, starting at one end of the sewn strip, cut narrow slits into the folded edge to make frilly petals, stopping just above the stitch line on the opposite edge. Do this all the way across the length of the strip. *(See illustration A.)*

To create a flower, start from one of the short edges and begin rolling the fabric into a spiral, holding along the sewn edge as you roll. Use a hand-sewing needle and thread to make hand stitches at the bottom edge of the rolled flower, through several layers, as you roll, to hold it all securely. *(See illustration B.)*

Vary the flowers by adding a contrasting center to some. Simply roll a smaller, shorter strip of one felt color first as described above, then continue rolling, using the main flower color, until you are done.

3) **Hot glue the flowers onto the mirror.** Queue up some inspiration in the form of peppy music, because this part is very fun! Add flowers around the mirror, stepping back and looking at the composition often. The flowers look nicest when they are in dense clusters, so don't be afraid to place them close together. In addition to adding the flowers, I also glued on small bunches of yarn tied together, and simple leaves cut from scrap fabric. Think of creative ways to fill in any space on the frame that needs a bit more.

4) **Hang and enjoy!** Add picture-hanging hardware to the back of the mirror, if needed.

A.

B.

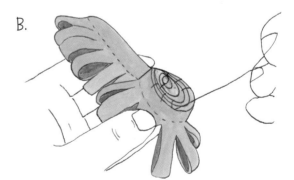

Leather-Covered Rocks

Nature is beautiful on its own, but sometimes it's fun to enhance or manipulate it with a little handcrafting. Not too long ago, in my father-in-law's office, I came upon one of the coolest things I've ever seen. A rock completely covered in leather sits on his desk; it had been purchased on a trip to Italy many years ago. It had a deep, coffee brown mottled surface, with a smoothness, sheen, and patina that can only come from years of handling and use. I spent the next few months trying to re-create that rock and think I finally achieved it, although another forty years on someone's desk will be the real deciding factor. These rocks are an unusual, tactile, and beautiful gift for someone's home or to use in an office. Larger rocks are good for paperweights, but smaller ones can be beautifully stacked on top of each other, channeling your inner Andy Goldsworthy. In a pinch, you could buy smooth flat rocks at the craft store, but part of the fun of this project is foraging and collecting the perfect ones. If you are buying leather specifically for this project, I suggest 3-to 5-ounce vegetable-tanned leather, from Tandy Leather.

MATERIALS:

Smooth, flat river rocks

Scrap leather (thinner leather works best)

Spray bottle filled with water

Large plastic bag

Contact cement (I used Tanner's Bond Craftsman #4085)

Leather dye (I used Eco-Flo All-In-One in colors Acorn Brown and Tan Prairie)

Leather finish liquid (I used Eco-Flo Satin Shene)

From the Crafter's Toolkit:

All-purpose cleaner and paper towels

Sharp scissors

Craft knife

Newspaper or drop cloth to protect work surface

Rubber gloves

TO MAKE:

1) **Prepare the rocks.** Clean and scrub the rocks thoroughly, and allow to dry completely.

2) **Prepare your leather.** Using scissors, cut two pieces of the leather a bit larger than half of your rock (speaking in terms of the top and bottom halves, not sides). Spray the cut leather pieces thoroughly on both sides with water (aim for thoroughly damp, but not saturated and dripping). Enclose these pieces in a plastic bag for at least 1 hour to allow the water to saturate and penetrate through the hide, which will help make the leather pliable.

3) Cover each half of the rock with the leather. Once the leather is evenly damp with water, pull it out of the plastic bag and gently give it a stretch in all directions; you will see that it will have some give and elasticity to it. Cover half of the rock completely with the contact cement and allow it to sit for 30 seconds, to become a bit tacky. Next, lay the leather piece over that side of the rock, starting at the middle, smoothing out the leather, stretching it a bit, and molding it completely to the rock, slowly moving from the center out toward the edge of this half of the rock. Take your time with this step and aim for a snug fit. Once you're satisfied with how this half looks, allow it to dry for 10 minutes or so before moving on. Trim off any excess leather and create an even edge, using a craft knife. You're now ready to cover the other half of the rock following the same procedure. (Tip: When painting the contact cement on the second half, be sure to paint it all the way up to the first side's edge, so the edge of the second side will stick well.) Allow this side to dry in the same manner before trimming the edge. When trimming the second half's edge, leave just a little excess, then push and press it into place against the other side's edge. Your goal is little to no gap between where the edges meet up, keeping in mind that the hide will shrink just a bit when it dries. Allow the covered rock to dry overnight before proceeding.

4) Dye and finish the rocks. Lay down newspaper or a drop cloth, to protect your work surface. Don the rubber gloves. Rub the leather dye all over the rock, following the dye's instructions. Rub off any excess dye, using a dry paper towel. To deepen the shade or to cover missed spots, go back over the rock a second time with the dye. Allow to dry according to the package instructions. Apply the leather finish in the same manner; allow to dry according to the package instructions.

OTHER IDEA:

* If you're feeling extra crafty, paint a small image on the leather, using acrylic craft paint.

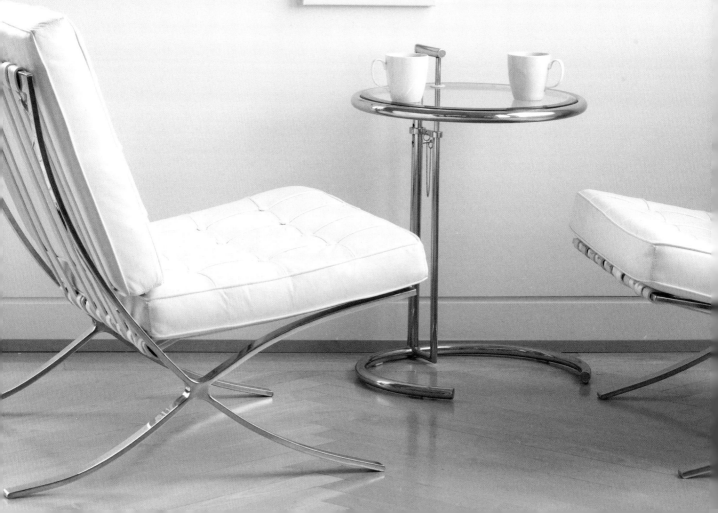

Glittered Art

Inspired by glitter artist Camomile Hixon, I wanted to create some original pieces of my own using made-up words (which we do a lot of in our family) and funny juxtapositions of seemingly "quiet" words. One night we discussed with the kids that we are not really hipsters, maybe more burbsters (can you picture it?). And what better way to declare you're an introvert than in big, glittery letters? Think outside the box, and hang these pieces where their sparkle will be maximized.

MATERIALS:

Blank canvases in desired shapes and sizes

Computer

Printer

Card stock–weight paper

Glitter

Spray clear-coat polyurethane with matte finish

From the Crafter's Toolkit:

Newspaper or drop cloth to protect work surface

Apron (glitter is messy)

Acrylic paint

Three paintbrushes of varying sizes

Craft knife and extra blades

Ruler

Pencil

Double-sided tape

Craft glue (I used Mod Podge)

TO MAKE:

1. **Prepare your canvas.** Protect your work surface, and don your apron. Prepare your canvas by painting it your desired background color. Allow it to dry thoroughly.

2. **Decide on and create your words.** I recommend large and simple fonts, but experiment with all sorts of lettering styles to figure out what you like best. Print them out onto card stock–weight paper. Using a craft knife, carefully cut out each of the letters.

3. **Transfer the words onto the canvas.** Lay the letters on your canvas, playing with placement until you're satisfied (a ruler is helpful for lining everything up). Use small pieces of double-sided tape to keep them the letters in place. Trace around each letter, using a well-sharpened pencil and keeping the lines around each letter light. Once you've traced the entire word, you can remove the cut letters.

4. **Time to glitter!** Okay, it's about to get fun. I found it easiest to glitter each letter individually and thoroughly. Paint the inside area of the letter, using the craft glue. Then sprinkle the area with glitter, and after a minute or so, tap to remove the excess. Repeat on all letters. (Tip: Tap the excess glitter onto a clean sheet of paper, then pour it back into the bottle when you're done, so none is wasted.)

5. **Touch up, if needed.** Touch up as needed by filling in where the coverage is light or areas you missed the first time as in the previous step. Allow the piece to dry flat for 24 hours. Lastly, give the piece a final tap, and then spray the entire canvas with a couple light coats of clear-coat polyurethane to protect it.

OTHER IDEA:

* Glitter the spaces around the letters instead of inside.

Pebble and Beach Glass Necklace

An elegant necklace to remind you of family beach walks. Once you collect the supplies to make these, plan on making several and giving them to those you love. Any type of beach glass, smooth pebble, or river rock would be ideal. Think about reusing beads from old jewelry. The necklaces in the photograph have a selection of freshwater pearls, small crystal beads, and various other findings.

MATERIALS:

Collected beach glass and pebbles (the ones in the photograph are each about 1 inch across)

24-gauge stainless-steel jewelry or artistic wire

Wire snips

Needle-nose pliers (very helpful to have two pairs, but you can work with one)

Spool of size 4 beige silk jewelry cord

Sterling silver hook-and-eye clasp set

Size 2 beading needle

Additional beads, if desired

From the Crafter's Toolkit:

Ruler

All-purpose scissors

Strong glue, such as Super Glue

TO MAKE:

1) Wrap the artistic wire around each beach glass or pebble to make a "setting." Snip off a 12-inch length of the wire (this is more than you will need, but the length makes it easier to work with). Bend the wire in half, marking the halfway point with a small bend. Place your collected piece at the marked bend, and using needle-nose pliers, wrap the wire snugly around the piece several times, using the photo as a guide. Wrap it securely, then bring the wire ends together at the top of the piece and twist them two or three times. Think of it as wrapping a twist tie around the opening of a bag (but more neatly, of course). With the extra wire at the top, you will fashion a loop for hanging, the ends of which will wrap a few more times around twisted area at the top of the piece. Snip off any extra wire, and tuck any pointy ends back into the wrapped areas.

2) String the beads. Cut 1 yard of silk cord for each necklace and attach one-half of the hook-and-eye clasp to one end of the cord. Do this by knotting the cord around the closure a few times and pulling snugly. Add a dot of Super Glue to the knot. Thread the beading needle onto the opposite end of the cord and begin constructing the necklace. At this point, you can begin to string on any beads or other embellishments you want to use. Experiment with different beading configurations. Keep checking the length as you add beads. Add the wire-wrapped collected glass in the middle of the stringing process, and be sure the bead pattern matches on both sides of it.

3) Trim and finish necklace. Once all the beads have been strung, trim the necklace to your desired length. Add the other half of the closure to the open end of the cord as described in Step 2.

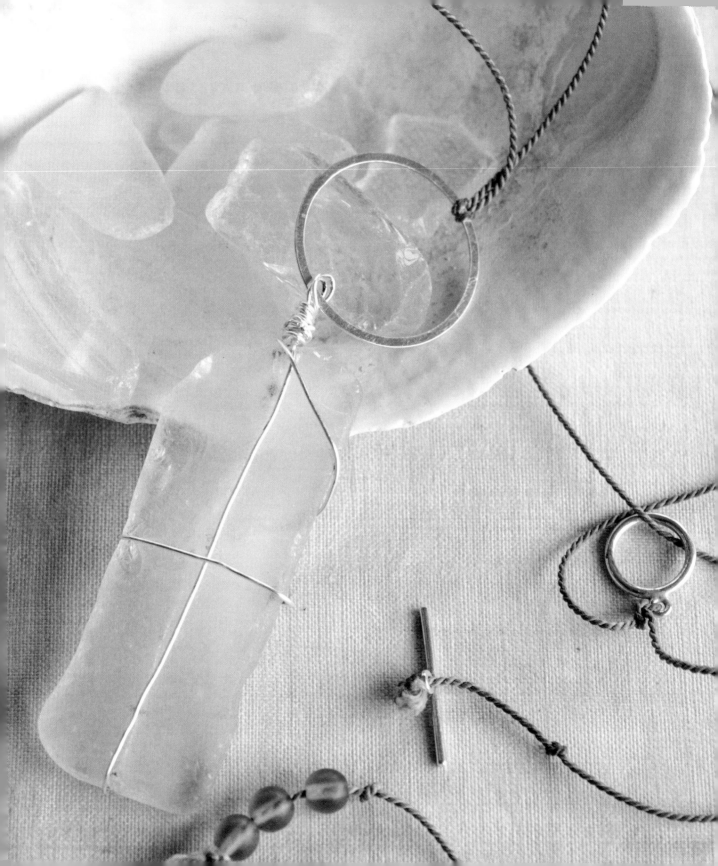

Hand-Loomed Place Mats

On my studio wall, I have weavings done by both of my kids. When I look at them, I think of their little first-grade fingers, busy with intense concentration, weaving those little swatches of cloth. There is something really satisfying about taking simple strips of fabric from a pair of frayed and tattered denim jeans and creating a useful, beautiful, unique piece of cloth like these place mats, each measuring about 18 x 14 inches. The end result is durable and washable (they were once jeans, after all). I used several shades of denim jeans my kids had outgrown, as well as some cream-colored corduroy pants and some scraps of suede I had in my fabric stash. Any fabric that can be hand washed and cut into strips can be used. A set of these makes a special and unique gift for friends . . . or yourself. Gather your materials, queue up your favorite movie or audio book, and start weaving.

MATERIALS:

A scrap piece of wood to create your loom, at least 20 x 16 inches (or you can repurpose an empty picture frame)

Old jeans or thick scrap fabric, (three pairs of kid's jeans will give you plenty of strips for a set of four place mats)

About 140 standard-size nails with small heads

1 ball of jute, kitchen twine, or a similarly strong string

Fork (optional)

Crochet hook

From the Crafter's Toolkit:

Yardstick or long ruler

Pencil

Hammer

Fabric scissors

Wide tape, for covering the rough edges of the loom (optional)

TO MAKE:

1) **Create the loom.**
On your wooden board or frame, measure out a 19½ x 15½-inch rectangle and mark with pencil. A standard place mat size is 18 x 14 inches; these are a little larger, but you decide what works best for you. Make marks in increments of ½ inch on all four sides of the rectangle. Hammer a nail onto each of these marks. (I found the edges of my board a little rough, and taped the sides with wide tape.) Position the board for weaving so that it is wider from side to side.

2) **Set up your loom.**
Using the jute, tie a knot around the first nail on the bottom left corner. Now bring the string up to the top left horizontal nail, loop around, go back down and loop around the next bottom nail, then back up to the next nail on the top row, and so on, until you have looped the string around each nail across the top and bottom of the rectangle. Knot off the string on the bottom right nail and trim away the excess. (This step does not have to be done super tightly; leave yourself room to weave.)

3) **Prepare your fabric strips.**
Cut away any bulky areas of the jeans (pockets, hems, etc). You will use primarily the fabric from the legs of the jeans. Cut the leg panels into roughly ½-inch strips. This does not have to be precise; in fact, varying the width can look more interesting.

Start the movie, if you haven't already.

45

4) **Begin your weaving.**
With the loom on your lap, or standing at a table, start at the bottom of the loom and begin weaving from the right to the left, going horizontally across the rectangle (leave a 2-inch tail at the beginning to tie off later). Weave over, under, over, under, and so on, until you get to the opposite end, at which point you will wrap the strip around the bottom nail on the left side and start across again. This time across, you'll alternate the over-under that you did on the first row (if you went under a piece of string, this time you will go over). Next time across, alternate again, and so on. (Tip: Weaving as densely and tightly as you can makes a much more substantial mat. Use your fingers or a fork to pull the strips together tightly after every few rows.) *(See illustration.)*

5) **To join a new strip of fabric to the current strip,** cut a ½-inch-wide lengthwise slit close to the edge at the end of the strip you're weaving with (essentially making a hole). Do the same at the beginning edge of the next strip. Insert the edge (with the slit) of the new strip through the slit in the current one, then thread the opposite end of the new strip through its own slit, to connect the strips together. Pull this to tighten and continue on.

6) **Finish the place mat.** The last few rows are the toughest to weave, and I found that a crochet hook was helpful to pull the strips around the string. Tie off the beginning and ending loose tails with a knot around the last nails. To remove the place mat from the loom, pull the string off each of the nails gently (a crochet hook can help with this, too).

Even though these place mats are made with machine-washable fabric, they are still hand loomed, and hand washing them in cold water will keep them in good shape.

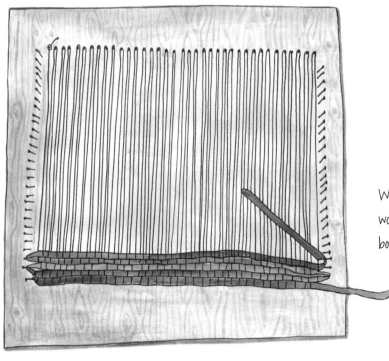

Weave strips across loom, working right to left, bottom to top.

Crocheted Treasure Bag

We are lucky to live only minutes from shorelines in every direction from our house in Seattle. If you see us there, likely our heads will be down, hunting for treasures in the sand. The idea for this bag came to me one day while carrying handfuls of sand-covered shells back to our car. Worn as a necklace around a child's neck, tied to the strap of a larger bag, or strung through a belt loop, it holds found treasures, while the open weave of the crochet stitches allows the sand to naturally sift out. When the hunt is over, the drawstring closure keeps everything safe.

Note: The bag itself is crocheted, but the handle to hang it from is knitted, my preferred method for a sturdy cord. Instructions for both a knitted I-cord and a crocheted handle follow. Choose the method you prefer; either will work. Gauge is not critical for this project, but using a slightly larger hook size than what your yarn recommends will allow for a more open weave, which will help the sand sift out.

MATERIALS:

Fingering-weight yarn (I used Habu Gima 100% cotton yarn, color 15)

Crochet hook, 2.00 to 2.75 mm (US size B to C)

6 locking stitch markers or scraps of contrast yarn

2 double-pointed knitting needles, 2.25 mm (US size 1) (optional)

From the Crafter's Toolkit:

Scissors

Yarn or tapestry needle

Abbreviations Used:

CH–chain

DC–double crochet

REV SC–reverse single crochet (also known as Crab Stitch Edging)

SC–single crochet

SL ST–slip stitch

TO MAKE:

The bag is crocheted in the round. You will be starting from the bottom of the bag, working up.

1)   Create the bottom of the bag. **CH** 6 and **SL ST** into the first **CH** to form a ring.

Round 1: **CH** 1, **SC** 12 into the center of the ring, **SL ST** into the first **SC** to join. (12 sts)

Round 2: **CH** 3, **DC** 1 into the first **SC** of the previous round (equals 2 **DC**), **DC** 2 into each **SC** from the previous round all the way around, **SL ST** into the third **CH** from the beginning to join. (24 sts)

Round 3: **CH** 1, **SC** 1 into each **DC** from the previous round, all the way around, **SL ST** into the first **SC** to join. (24 sts)

Round 4: **CH** 3, **DC** 1 into the first **SC** of the previous round (equals 2 **DC**), **DC** 2 into each **SC** from the previous round all the way around, **SL ST** into the third **CH** from the beginning to join. (48 sts)

Round 5: **CH** 1, **SC** 1 into each **DC** from the previous round all the way around, **SL ST** into the first **SC** to join. (48 sts)

Round 6: **CH** 3, **DC** 1 into the next **SC** from the previous round (equals 2 **DC**), *DC 1 in the next 2 **SC**, **DC** 2 in the next **SC***, repeat from * to * all the way around, **SL ST** into the third **CH** from the beginning. (64 sts)

Rounds 7–9: **CH** 1, **SC** into every stitch from the previous round all the way around, **SL ST** into the first **SC** to join. (64 sts)

2) Make the sides of the bag.

Round 10: ***CH** 3, skip the first **SC** from the previous round, **SC** into the next **SC***. Repeat from * to * all the way around. (32 "loops") Place a locking stitch marker (or use a piece of contrast scrap yarn) to mark the beginning of the round.

Rounds 11–35: ***CH** 3, **SC** into the **CH**-3 space from the previous round*. Repeat from * to * all the way around. (32 "loops")

Round 36: **CH** 1, **SC** 2 into each loop space from the previous round all the way around, **SL ST** into the first **SC** to join. (64 sts)

Rounds 37–40: **CH** 1, **SC** in every **ST** from the previous round all the way around, **SL ST** into the first **SC** to join. (64 sts). Remove the stitch marker.

3) Make the top edge of the bag.

Round 41: Begin the Reverse Single Crochet (**REV SC**) edging. Insert your hook into the first stitch from the previous round, make 1 **SC**. *Working from left to right (instead of right to left), insert the hook into the next stitch to the right (from the previous round) and **SC**.* Repeat from * to * all the way around, **SL ST** to the first **SC** to join. Fasten off the yarn, weave in the ends.

4) Make the loops to hold the handle. Place six locking stitch markers evenly spaced around the top of the bag.

To make one loop: **SC** 3 into the same space as a stitch marker.

Row 1: **CH** 10.

Row 2 and 3: **CH** 1, **SC** into the second stitch from the hook, **SC** in every **CH** from the previous row.

Attach the end of the loop to the bag: **SC** 3 in the space beside the stitch marker space. Fasten off the yarn. Weave in the ends.

Repeat for each loop to make a total of six.

5) Make the handle.

To make a crocheted handle:

Row 1: Chain stitch a length measuring about 35 inches long.

Row 2 and 3: **CH** 1, **SC** into each chain from the previous row.

Fasten off the yarn. Thread the handle through the six loops and sew the two ends together, using the same yarn and a yarn needle. Weave in the ends.

To make a knitted I-cord handle:

Using two double-pointed knitting needles and the same yarn, cast on six stitches.

Knit each stitch. At the end of this and every row, do not turn your work. Instead, slide the row across the needle to the other side and, bringing the working yarn across the back of those stitches, continue knitting each stitch. Repeat from * to * until the cord measures 35 inches (or your desired length). Bind off.

Thread the I-cord through the six loops and sew the two ends together, using the same yarn and a yarn needle. Weave in the ends.

Pinpoint Oxford Eiderdown Coverlet

This is the perfect bit of extra warmth to pull out in early spring when there's still a bit of chill in the air. Inspired by a traditional English eiderdown, it has two layers of batting to create a cozy cover to throw over cold toes (or over a sleeping child when Mom has put the flannel sheets away a little too soon). The Pinpoint Oxford cloth used for high-quality men's dress shirts is a gorgeously fine fabric, wonderful to sew with. I focused on three main colors (white, pale blue, and a darker blue), but chose shade and weave variations within each of those colors for added surface interest. As a rule of thumb, each shirt will yield about twenty-five 4½-inch squares. I chose neutral colors that would work anywhere in our house, but it would also be beautiful done in stripes, checks, or bold prints.

The finished size is 48 inches square. This is a great size to use as a top layer for a child's crib or as a lap blanket, but you can easily make a larger or smaller quilt by simply adding or subtracting rows.

MATERIALS:

6 men's Pinpoint Oxford cloth shirts in varying colors and textures

1 twin-size cotton bedsheet, for backing

2 packages crib-size high-loft quilt batting, between ½ and ¾ inch thick (I used Soft n Crafty Poly-Fil Extra-Loft batting, 45 x 60 inches)

1 skein size 8 perle cotton embroidery thread in a complementary color (you could also use wool or cotton yarn)

Audio books: This project is a great time to catch up!

From the Crafter's Toolkit:

Iron and ironing board

Fabric scissors

Quilter's clear ruler

Rotary cutter and self-healing cutting mat

Painter's blue tape

Straight pins

Sewing machine and coordinating thread

Size 3 or 4 upholstery needle with a sharp tip

Hand-sewing needle

TO MAKE:

1) **Prepare the shirts and sheet.** Wash, dry, and press all the shirts and the bedsheet you'll use for the back. Set aside the bedsheet for now.

2) **Cut squares.** Cut away the collars, cuffs, pockets, and seams from the shirt. From the panels that are left, cut 4½-inch squares, using your quilter's clear ruler, rotary cutter, and cutting mat. I used fifty squares of whites, fifty of light blues, and fifty of darker blues.

3) **Lay out your design.** Working in rows from left to right and top to bottom, following the illustration, lay out the patchwork pattern. (Tip: It's nice to have a cleared floor space or large table for this step.) Distribute any variations within each color range through-out the pattern so there is a nice flow of colors across the coverlet. If you need to move this project before the top is sewn together, stack each row from right to left in order (placing next square on top), labeling each stack with painter's blue tape: "Row 1," "Row 2," and so on. Pin or clip each row together.

4) **Sew the squares into rows.** Machine sew the squares together one row at a time with the right sides together and using a ¼-inch seam allowance. It helps to lay out each row again after you've sewn it to double check the patchwork pattern. Press all seam allowances open.

5) **Sew the rows together.** Starting with the top two rows, right sides facing, pin well, matching up each square's seamlines. Machine sew lengthwise across the rows, using a ¼-inch seam allowance, and press the seam allowances open. Continue doing this until you've pieced the top completely. The coverlet top is now complete.

6) **Sew the patchwork front to the backing sheet.** Trim down the backing sheet so it's the same size as the patchwork front, which should be 48½ inches square. Lay the patchwork top on your backing sheet, right sides together. Pin and sew along three of the four sides, just as if you're sewing a large pillowcase, using a ¼-inch seam allowance. Trim away the excess fabric at the corners to ease bulk and turn right side out, gently pushing corners out.

7) **Insert the batting into the "pillowcase."** Cut two layers of batting to measure 45 inches square (trimming the batting a bit smaller compensates for the extra bulk it has). Place both layers on top of each other, smoothing them out. Slip the layers into the cover through the open side. Take your time; this can be a bit fussy. (Tip: It helped me to match up a corner of the batting layers, once they were inside, with a corner of the cover, and pin those together to hold them while I worked on the other side.)

Once all the layers are stacked and in place, pin together: Starting in the center of the quilt top and moving outward, place a pin in the middle of each square, going through all the layers.

8) **Tie the layers together.** Thread the upholstery needle with perle cotton thread or yarn. Working from the back to front of the coverlet, bring the needle up at each corner where four squares meet. Make a ¼- to ½-inch-long diagonal stitch across that seam, pushing the needle back through to the back. Tie with a square knot on the back, leaving 3-inch tails. Do this over the entire coverlet.

9) **Finish the coverlet.** To close the open end, fold in a ¼-inch seam allowance, press lightly, and pin the edges together. Slipstitch closed by hand stitching with coordinating thread.

OTHER IDEAS:

* Leave in interesting details from the original shirts, such as the pockets, button placket, or cuffs.

* Use a collection of shirts that belonged to a loved one to create a special memory quilt.

CHAPTER TWO

SUMMER

Deep summer is when laziness finds respectability. —SAM KEEN

Sand on the floor makes no difference at our house in summer: we have all but moved outdoors for a few months. Celebrations, reunions, impromptu get-togethers, bridal showers, weddings are all in season. Days seem endless and afternoons are wonderfully idle at our house. There's suddenly time for board games and art projects. It's the time of year the adults can call cocktails and finger foods "dinner."

It's also the peak season for garage sales. I always keep a list of what I'm looking for with me, which right now includes white bowls, interesting dishes, oil paintings, and vintage fabric.

Trinket Bowls p.59

Vintage Decal Kitchen Pieces p.60

Hunted and Gathered Posies p.63

Doily Tees p.64

Renewed Chair Seats p.66

Updated Oil Paintings p.68

Summer Bloom
Specimen Jars p.71

Custom Patched Jeans p.72

Found Crystal Bracelets p.75

Summer Pillow Jackets p.76

Woven Chair Back p.79

Hand-Painted Journals p.80

Bead-Bombed Tote Bag p.83

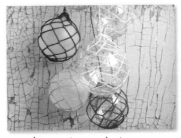

Glass Fishing Floats p.87

Summer Sherbet Picnic Blanket p.90

Trinket Bowls

This is a modern "pinch pot" that is pretty enough to sit at party table or to hold rings, earrings, and other small jewelry items. A 2-ounce bar of clay will yield two bowls, each measuring about 1 inch tall by 3½ inches in diameter. (Note: If you plan to use your bowls for food items, be sure to use clay labeled as food-safe.)

MATERIALS:

White oven-bake clay (I used Sculpey)

Rolling pin

Oven-safe bowls about 3½ inches in diameter, to use as a form

Small knife

Parchment paper

Baking sheet

Oven

From the Crafter's Toolkit:

Sandpaper

Acrylic craft paint

Small paintbrush

TO MAKE:

1) **Prepare the clay.** Break off a 1-ounce block of clay and work it in your hands until it's warm and pliable. Lay it on your work surface, then use a rolling pin to roll out smooth and flat to a thickness of about ⅛ inch. Turn the piece often to keep it from sticking and roll it into a circular shape.

2) **Create the bowl shape.** Turn your bowl upside down and lay the circle of clay evenly over the bottom of it. Gently smooth out the clay, making your bowl at least 1 inch tall. Using a knife, cut away the excess around the edges of the clay bowl and create a straight-ish bowl rim.

3) **Bake the piece.** While still on the bowl, bake on a parchment-lined baking sheet in the oven, according to the package instructions. Allow it to cool down a bit before handling.

4) **Finish the bowl.** Remove the clay bowl from the glass gently, by pulling evenly all around. If needed, gently sand the rim of the bowl to smooth it up.

5) **Decorate the bowl.** Use acrylic paint and a paintbrush to add small details of color to the bowl.

Vintage Decal Kitchen Pieces

The Meyercord Decal Company produced water-slide transfer decals that were widely popular with housewives of the 1940s and '50s who wanted to add their own creative twist to things around their home. You can still find quite a good selection of them today; a quick search on eBay or Etsy.com for "Meyercord decal" yields a long list of decal flowers, animals, and patterns at reasonable prices. Add them to all kinds of rescued pieces from the thrift store. My husband even has a Meyercord rooster decal on the back of his motorcycle helmet. (Note: These pieces are for decoration only.)

MATERIALS:

Meyercord decals

Items you want to add transfers to (can be wood, ceramic, or glass)

A bowl of warm water

Clean sponge

Spray clear-coat polyurethane (I used Krylon Clear Polyurethane)

From the Crafter's Toolkit:

Paper scissors

Cloth or paper towels

TO MAKE:

1) **Prepare and apply your decals.** If you receive your Meyercord decals in their original packaging, follow the instructions provided. Cut out the decal you want to transfer, immerse it in warm water until it begins to release from the paper (usually 20 to 30 seconds), and then carefully slide the decal onto the surface and off the paper. Do this step slowly as these decals can be delicate because of their age. Carefully position the decal where you want it.

2) **Smooth out any wrinkles.** Using a sponge, gently press out any bubbles so the decal lies smoothly. Use a cloth or paper towel to carefully dry any excess water. Allow to dry completely.

3) **Finish the piece.** Spray the surface with a couple of light coats of clear-coat polyurethane spray to protect it and seal the decal onto it.

Hunted and Gathered Posies

Pinned to a purse or the lapel of a coat, placed in a glass vase, or tied to a gift, these will always make someone smile. I made mine of miscellaneous small trinkets collected from my jewelry box and craft shelves.

MATERIALS:

Beaded jewelry, interesting trims, beautiful buttons, silk flowers, lace, small paper doilies

Floral or 20- to 22-gauge craft wire

Ruler

Green floral tape

Scraps of ribbon (optional)

Pin backs (I used 1½-inch Darice nickel-plated) (optional)

From the Crafter's Toolkit:

All-purpose scissors

Hot glue gun

TO MAKE:

1) **Make stems for your pieces.** Create a stem on each of the pieces by threading a piece of floral wire through its bottom or by wrapping wire around it. With the item at the center of a 12-inch length of wire, fold each side of the wire down to create the stem, twist the wire together a few times, and trim to your desired length. (Tip: Anything you can't thread wire through can be hot glued to a bit of wire, or perhaps, inconspicuously, to something else in the posy.)

2) **Arrange your pieces.** Start grouping your stems into a posy. Once you have a grouping you like, hold the stems together firmly as one stem, and use the green floral tape to wrap around them tightly to create one stem. Tie a ribbon around it, if desired.

3) **How to create a posy pin.** To use as a pin, apply the pin back with hot glue, running vertically up and down the back of the stem.

Doily Tees

I challenged myself to create something new out of a collection of secondhand and orphaned cloth doilies I found one day. I realized there is so much that can be created around the open-weave patterning of a doily. Cut out and around the interesting bits, hand sew them with brightly colored embroidery thread onto plain T-shirts, and they suddenly look completely new and original.

MATERIALS:

Doilies (I used crocheted cotton and woven cotton ones)

T-shirts

Fray Stop (optional)

Embroidery floss in several contrasting colors (I used DMC)

From the Crafter's Toolkit:

Iron and ironing board

Straight pins

Fabric scissors

Embroidery needle

TO MAKE:

1) **Prepare materials.** Prewash the doilies with the T-shirts to be sure everything can be laundered together in the end. Let dry completely, then press the doilies and T-shirt. (Tip: If your doilies are quite misshapen and crumpled straight out of the dryer, you can pin them back in their original shape directly to your ironing board surface as you steam press them.)

2) **Plan out your design.** Look at the patterning of each doily: What areas can you stitch through and around? Decide where it will be placed on the shirt. Carefully cut out the areas of the doily you will be using on your design, and pin onto the T-shirt. The doily edges should not fray or ravel with careful cutting, but if they do, apply Fray Stop.

3) **Embroider the doily to the T-shirt.** Contrast the color of embroidery floss in different areas to create a secondary pattern. If using DMC embroidery floss, separate the six strands of floss into two sets of three strands each; you will sew with three strands.

Begin hand stitching the doily onto the T-shirt, keeping in mind that you are making a design with your thread as you stitch. One of the doilies I used (shown on the pink T-shirt) had a circle pattern with small eyelets that worked really well with little X stitches.

Continue stitching, making sure your embroidery stitches completely secure the doily to the T-shirt. Stitch around the edge of the doily, if needed, for extra stability. Repeat for additional doilies and shirts.

OTHER IDEA:

* Add a hand-sewn label for the inside neck. Embroider simple letters by using a backstitch onto a doily scrap, or write with a permanent marker onto a scrap of fabric, then stitch down on all four sides (keeping in mind the stitches will show on the back of the shirt, which I like the look of).

Renewed Chair Seats

I knew I could pretty up these four thrift store chairs with a little paint and new seat fabrics, and I love that their different back shapes still show up so nicely. Consider using chairs like this outside for a summer party, and don't worry if they get stained (now that you know how easy it is to redo them). Maybe some new orange seats for Halloween. Consider redoing what you already have, or look for well-made chairs to minimize the amount of repairs you will have to make. Tightening screws is one thing, but if one leg is wonky or broken, it can easily turn into a bigger job. Working outside with a little music makes this project fun.

MATERIALS:

Wooden chairs with drop-in upholstered seats

4 bricks

Latex paint

Pliers

Fabric, for the seats

Fabric, for lining the seats (e.g., muslin)

Quilt batting (I used Warm & Natural)

Foam cushioning (optional)

Serrated knife

Staple gun and staples

From the Crafter's Toolkit:

Screwdriver

Sandpaper

All-purpose cleaner and cloth

Newspaper or drop cloth to protect work surface

Paintbrushes

Fabric scissors

Black marker (optional)

TO MAKE:

1) **Remove the seat and prepare the chair.** Usually, the seat is attached with four screws on the underside corners. Set the entire seat aside, but save the screws. Give the wood frame a light, allover sanding and clean thoroughly. Spread newspaper or a drop cloth to protect your work surface, raise the legs up onto bricks, and give the chair a couple of light coats of paint. Allow to dry.

2) **Remove the old seat cover completely.** It's helpful to pull the old staples out with a pair of pliers. Use the old cover as a template to cut the fabric, lining fabric, and batting pieces for the new cover. (Tip: A good rule of thumb is that the fabric, lining fabric, and batting should be at least 5 inches larger on all sides than the size of the seat, to allow them to wrap around the sides.)

Is the foam on the seat still usable? If not, cut a new piece of foam. To measure, trace the wooden seat bottom onto the new foam piece, using a black marker, and cut, using a serrated knife.

3) **Attach the new seat cover.** On your work surface, lay out the following stack of layers: the wooden seat bottom, cut foam, layer of quilt batting, lining fabric, and main fabric, each right side up. To begin stapling, flip the entire stack over, pull all layers firmly around to the back of the wooden seat at the middle of one side, and staple once. Do the same thing on the opposite side (still pulling firmly). Next do the remaining two sides. Continue pulling and stapling firmly on all four sides. Keep your staples about ½ inch apart. Fold the corners neatly and uniformly. Staple down. Screw the finished seat onto the chair.

OTHER IDEA:

* Try painting your own design or pattern directly onto the fabric, similar to the hand-painted journal project on page 80, before stapling it to the seat. Use fabric paints instead of acrylic.

Updated Oil Paintings

Having oil portraits painted of children was popular where I grew up in central North Carolina; maybe that's why I love them so. I'm always on the lookout for interesting secondhand original oil paintings, and I picked up these two for ten dollars each. An afternoon of sprucing up and they are beautifully original again.

MATERIALS:

Framed oil painting

Spray paint

Enameled jewelry, pearls, extra beads and crystals left over from other projects, craft store birds, or any other kind of trim that could be used on the painting

Scrap fabric (optional)

Picture-hanging hardware (optional)

From the Crafter's Toolkit:

Newspaper or drop cloth to protect work surface

All-purpose cleaner and cloth

Painter's blue tape

Sandpaper

Face mask

Rubber gloves

Apron

Acrylic craft paints

Paintbrushes

Hot glue gun

Fabric scissors

Craft glue (I used Mod Podge) (optional)

TO MAKE:

1) **Lay down newspaper or a drop cloth to protect your work surface.** Thoroughly clean and lightly sand the picture frame. Use newspaper to cover the picture and tape it off completely. Don the face mask, rubber gloves, and apron. Apply several light coats of spray paint to the frame and allow to dry thoroughly.

2) **Spruce up the painting.** The colors of the original paintings I found were a little drab, perhaps from sun fading or age, and I wanted to brighten them up and unify them visually, as they would be hanging together. Using acrylic craft paint and brushes, I just added a little color here and there, whitening the teeth, brightening the darkest flowers, changing the shade of the yellow flowers a bit. A few alterations made a big difference.

3) **Add dimensional embellishments.** Using a hot glue gun, add dimensional embellishments, such as enamel jewelry pieces, beads from an old necklace, a pair of earrings (with the backs cut off), and flocked birds from the craft store.

4) **Embellish the frame (optional).** If you want to add to the frame, glue on fabric trim as I did on one of mine. Simply cut a small strip of a pretty fabric and apply with craft glue around the frame. Allow to dry.

    Add picture-hanging hardware, if needed, and hang your new masterpiece.

Summer Bloom Specimen Jars

I am drawn to anything encased in glass, especially organic objects, such as butterflies and bugs. Give me a day at a natural history museum to stare at things under glass until closing time and I'm happy. I created these specimen jars by repurposing beverage glasses, turning them upside down to encase a flower or other object. A group of these make a simple, beautiful display from inexpensive market flowers (and the bonus is that our kitty can't get at them). I've also used these to display my heart-shaped rock collection or the special shells my kids collect. Once you gather the materials to make these, you'll want to make several.

MATERIALS:

Clear drinking glasses (with opening large enough to admit what is to be displayed inside)

Heavy cardboard or chipboard

Stuffing or scraps of quilt batting

Scraps of fabric

Small bulldog or binder clips

Craft felt (optional)

From the Crafter's Toolkit:

Pencil

All-purpose scissors

Craft glue (I used Elmer's)

TO MAKE:

1) **Make the base.** Wash and dry the glasses. Trace the mouth of each glass, using a pencil, onto two different pieces of scrap cardboard. Cut out both circles just a bit larger than their traced line, so your circle base will be slightly larger than the mouth of the glass. (You want the mouth of the glass to sit on its cardboard base, not over it.)

2) **Cut out two circles of fabric, both at least ½ inch larger than the cardboard base.** Using one of the cardboard bases, apply glue to one side in a very thin layer. Lay a fabric circle, right side down, on your work surface and center the cardboard base on it, glue side down. Wrap the extra fabric around to the back of the cardboard circle and glue it down. (Tip: Cut small notches into the edge of the fabric all the way around before wrapping it.) Hold everything in place with bulldog clips and allow to dry.

3) **Make the top portion of the base.** Glue a wad of quilt batting or stuffing to the center of one side of the second cardboard base. Lay the second fabric circle right side down on your work surface. Lay the cardboard circle, batting side down, on the center of the fabric. Glue fabric to base as in Step 2 using bulldog clips to hold the edges together. Allow to dry.

4) **Finish the base.** Once the two base parts are dry, glue their wrong sides together. Hold with bulldog clips until dry. To display flowers, snip the stem close to the flower itself, and lay on the base side with the raised center.

   Optionally, you can cut a circle of coordinating felt (slightly smaller than finished circles) and glue to the bottom, for a more finished look.

Custom Patched Jeans

Take a great-fitting pair of jeans and make them one-of-a-kind with fabric patches sewn onto worn or not-so-worn spots, attaching it all with some contrast embroidery stitches. This is a great carry-along project for summer vacations; just throw them in your bag and stitch by the pool. You can even wear them while they are a work in progress.

MATERIALS:

Pair of jeans

Variety of colorful fabric scraps

Double-sided fusible web (I used Pellon Wonder Under)

Embroidery floss in several coordinating colors (I used DMC)

From the Crafter's Toolkit:

Iron and ironing board

FriXion pen or water-soluble fabric marker

Fabric scissors

Straight pins

Hand-sewing needle

Thimble

TO MAKE:

1) **Wash and press the jeans.**

2) **Plan your design.** Lay the jeans out flat on your work surface to plan where you will place patches and add hand-stitched details. Such areas as a coin pocket, waistband, leg hems, and pocket openings are all good places to add color and interest. Fabric patches can be placed anywhere on the legs or back pockets, or over small pockets and belt loops. If needed, mark these areas with either a light pen mark or a straight pin. Flip the jeans over and do the same thing on the back.

3) **Create the fabric patches.** To make these, iron double-sided fusible web to the back of the fabric scraps, following the package directions. (Tip: I found it easiest to cut larger squares of the web, iron the fusible web onto the back of the fabric, then cut that piece into the shapes of the patches I needed.) Adhere each patch by removing the paper backing, laying the piece right side up on the pants, and pressing with an iron.

4) **Add stitching.** Even though you are fusing the patches onto the jeans, you will also add embroidery stitches around the patches, for reinforcement as well as for added embellishment. If using DMC embroidery floss, separate the six strands of floss into two sets of three strands each, and sew with three strands at a time. Hand stitch a simple running stitch around the edge of the patches.

Add more interest to your jeans by stitching a contrast running stitch around the pocket openings, at the hem or belt loops, or on the back pocket.

OTHER IDEAS:

* Create a holiday pair of jeans (or even a jacket) with sparkly or velvet fabric.

* Use this same patching method on shoes, bags, and skirts.

Found Crystal Bracelets

Throw one of these beauties on with a pair of jeans or a sundress, and you have the perfect amount of sparkle for a summer party. Half the fun of making these is foraging for the beads to use. Any bead or trinket that has a hole or two to sew through will work. I had a specific color scheme in mind, so I supplemented my found trinkets with ones from my favorite bead shop (see Resources). As a general rule of thumb, plan on about six larger beads, twelve medium-size beads, and twenty smaller ones to cover the top of the wrist; double that to cover the entire wrist.

MATERIALS:

About ½ yard ribbon

Assorted sew-on crystals, beads, and pearls in various sizes and colors (see headnote)

Buttons or other sentimental trinkets

Small seed beads to fill in between the larger beads (optional)

Size 10 beading needle

From the Crafter's Toolkit:

Ruler

All-purpose scissors

Pencil

Thread

The next television series on your list that you want to get lost in. *Downton Abbey* helped inspire and entertain me while I was making these bracelets.

TO MAKE:

1) **Cut and mark the ribbon.** Cut a length of ribbon 20 inches long. Faintly mark the ribbon's lengthwise midpoint with a pencil. Next, make a faint mark 3 inches on either side of the midpoint. This 6-inch length is the area of the bracelet you will cover with beads.

2) **Sew on the beads.** Set up a comfortable sewing area (perhaps with a cup of tea). Sew the larger beads onto the marked length of the ribbon first, spacing them along it randomly. Once you've sewn these on, do the same thing with the medium-size beads, and then the small beads. Lastly, if you want to fill in the ribbon even more, sew on tiny seed beads. This step isn't necessary, but I loved the finished look this step gave to the bracelets.

3) **Adorn your wrist!** To attach to the wrist, simply tie the ribbon in a bow. (By this time you should be engrossed in your chosen series, so have the supplies ready to make several bracelets.)

OTHER IDEA:

* Add beads to a flower from the Recycled Flower Mirror project (page 35) and add to these bracelets.

Pillow Jackets

At our house, pillows are the decor items I play around with when I want to change things up a bit. When I found a remnant of this flowery fabric with lots of cutwork and pops of pink at the thrift store, I kind of squealed—new pillows! As an oddly shaped piece, there wasn't quite enough to make full pillow covers. But we handcrafters know that problems like this are really opportunities in disguise. I realized I had just enough to make a few pillow jackets, essentially a tube of fabric sewn up and slipped over the pillow's existing cover. The color of the original pillow cover showing through the cutwork creates a lovely effect. Look for drapery fabrics, beautifully patterned blankets, and upholstery fabrics. Consider upcycling a pretty skirt or dress you no longer wear.

MATERIALS:

Square or rectangular pillow with a solid cover

A piece of pretty fabric able to go around the middle of your pillow (e.g., if your pillow measures 18 inches square, you would need a length of at least 36 ½ inches to wrap around your pillow)

From the Crafter's Toolkit:

Iron and ironing board

Tape measure

Pencil

Quilter's clear ruler

Rotary cutter and self-healing cutting mat

Straight pins

Sewing machine and coordinating thread

TO MAKE:

1) Prewash and iron the fabric.

2) **Measure and cut.** Measure around the middle of the pillow, keeping in mind you'll want a pillow jacket that's not too snug or loose. Add ½ inch for seam allowances, to get the total length for your fabric. To calculate the desired width, first decide how much of the cover you will want showing on either side of the jacket (for example, on the larger rectangular pillow pictured, I planned for 5 inches of the pillow fabric to show on either side of the jacket). Record this measurement and add 1 inch for seams. Cut the fabric panel based on these calculations, using a quilter's clear ruler, rotary cutter, and cutting mat.

3) **Sew the pillow jacket.** Hem each of the long edges of the pillow jacket by turning down ¼ inch to the wrong side of the fabric and press. Repeat to enclose the raw edge. Pin and machine stitch.

   Sew the short ends of the fabric together, right sides facing, using a ¼-inch seam allowance. Press the seam allowances open, turn the tube right side out, and press.

4) **Center the tube over the pillow and you're done.**

Woven Chair Back

I am not one of those lucky people who happen upon a set of midcentury modern dining chairs on the side of the road, although I have found interesting ones. Sometimes what seems blah at first glance just needs an open mind and a little love to be completely transformed. I found the caned back of this chair interesting and loved the patina of the wood, so home with me it came. By weaving stash yarn and strips of fabric through the caned back, this has now become my favorite chair. The weaving can take some time (four episodes of This American Life, *when I counted), but the rhythm of the process can really clear your mind. Or you could always put the kids to work.*

MATERIALS:

Scrap yarn or string

Chair with caning or something that will lend itself to weaving

Fabric cut into 1-inch-wide strips

From the Crafter's Toolkit:

All-purpose scissors

Tapestry needle with a large eye

TO MAKE:

1) **Weave the yarn and fabric strips.** Using a length of yarn threaded through a tapestry needle, begin on the bottom back of the caned area (I left the ends hanging on the back because I like the look, but you could knot and trim them off). Weave the yarn through the caning, creating an even pattern using any type of embroidery stitch you wish (backstitch, cross stitch, running stitch). Weave the fabric strips, using the same method. Alternate between weaving with fabric and yarn all the way across the chair back.

OTHER IDEA:

* Appliqué squares of fabric directly to the front of the chair back or to the seat (as shown in the photo), for another layer of pattern. Just cut squares and sew them onto the caning from the front, directly on top of the weaving.

Hand-Painted Journals

My children are prolific artists, and I am always looking for new ways to preserve their art and give it as a gift. Journals are something that many people use, so why not make the cover a piece of original art? These would be unique wedding or party guest books, to give grandparents, or for a child to paint and enjoy for themselves. But don't let the kids have all the fun. My sister-in-law Jenny painted a cluster of flowers and a sun-drenched landscape on pieces of fabric that became the journals you see here. I have provided instructions for two journal sizes: 8½ x 11 inches, and a 7½ x 9-inch more portable size.

Note: Measurements for the smaller size will be given in parentheses ( ) when necessary.

MATERIALS:

¼ yard solid fabric to paint (e.g., home decor weight or a midweight canvas)

Chipboard, such as shirt-size gift boxes (enough to make 2 l ayers of the full cover size)

Bulldog or binder clips

Heavy book

Filler paper (e.g., a pad of blank newsprint paper)

Awl or book board punch

1 yard ribbon, leather cording, or twine

From the Crafter's Toolkit:

Newspaper or drop cloth to protect work surface

Apron

Iron and ironing board

Ruler

All-purpose scissors

Acrylic paints in your choice of colors

Assorted sizes of paintbrushes

Pencil

Craft knife

Self-healing cutting mat

Craft glue (I used Mod Podge)

Size 9 crewel embroidery needle (optional)

TO MAKE:

1) **Paint the fabric cover.** Lay down newspaper or a drop cloth to protect your work surface, and don your apron. Iron the fabric, then cut a piece to measure 18½ by 12 inches (10½ by 9 inches). Paint your image onto the right side of the fabric. Have some fun and let your creative spirit really fly with this step, keeping in mind that filling the space will have the biggest impact. Allow to dry flat and undisturbed for 24 hours before proceeding to the next step. Measure and trim the painted fabric by ½ inch on all sides.

2) **Cut and glue the chipboard for the cover.** On the chipboard, mark the dimensions of the following pieces and cut out, using the craft knife and self-healing mat.

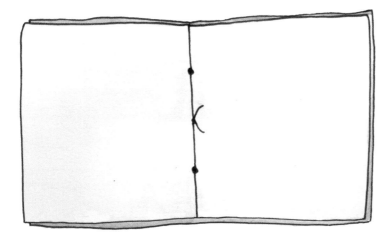

Outside cover:
17½ x 11 inches (11 x 9 inches).

Inside cover:
17 x 10½ inches (10½ x 8½ inches).

Using a paintbrush, paint one side of the outside cover piece of chipboard completely with craft glue. Place your fabric wrong side up on your protected work surface. Lay the glued side of the chipboard onto the fabric, centering it on all four sides. Press all over well to adhere. Allow the glue to begin to set for a minute or so, then paint a ½-inch strip of glue along all the edges of the chipboard side. Snugly fold the edges of the fabric over the edge of the chipboard on all sides, holding in place with bulldog clips. Allow to dry.

Completely cover one side of the inside cover piece of chipboard with craft glue, then position, glue side down, over the inside of the front cover centered on all four sides, and press. It should just cover the raw edges of the fabric. As before, hold in place with bulldog clips. Allow cover to dry overnight. (Tip: If the chipboard doesn't lie flat, place a heavy book over it while it's drying.)

3) **Cut the filler paper.** Decide how many sheets of paper your book will hold (each of mine holds forty sheets). Cut stacks of blank newsprint paper to 17 x 10½ inches (10½ x 8½ inches).

4) **Make holes in the cover for the binding.** Find the exact center of the width of the cover; this is where you will be folding the entire book in half. With a pencil, mark three evenly spaced points on the length of that midpoint. Create a hole at each of those points with an awl or a book board punch tool. Carefully fold the cover in half, creasing through the holes. Mark the three holes you made onto a scrap sheet of paper to use as a template for the filler paper.

Stack the paper neatly and place the template over the very center of the paper. Punch holes, using the method described. Fold all the pages in half.

5) **Assemble the book.** Lay the opened cover, right side down, on your work surface, and top with the filler paper. Using a crewel needle, if necessary, insert ribbon, twine, or leather cording through the top and bottom holes, from the inside of the book, and pull through to the outside. Next, insert both ends of the cord through the center hole back to the inside of the book and pull through. Tie a knot inside the book and clip away any excess *(see illustration)*.

OTHER IDEA:

* Go one step further and illustrate the borders of the filler paper

Bead-Bombed Tote Bag

"Yarn bombing" is a term for using yarn—knitted or crocheted pieces—to add colorful graffiti to urban areas, and this is a spin on that idea. Think of it as adding a little urban sparkle, one crystal at a time. I started with a pretty floral tablecloth that had seen a few too many messy meals, and then glued on some sparkly beads to match the colors in the floral pattern. For my bag I used 8 to 11 mm seed beads, and 3 to 6 mm bugle beads, all in various colors. Decide whether you want to mimic the colors of the area you're beading very closely, or vary the effect by going darker or lighter. An afternoon of gluing while quizzing my daughter on her Spanish vocabulary, and I have a new tote.

A few notes: The finished size is about 16½ inches tall, 14 inches wide, and 3¾ inches deep; the handle length is 12 inches. This tote is constructed with the seam allowances at the side seams showing on the outside of the bag. Also, the required cotton canvas does two things: It adds stability and just the right amount of stiffness, all to help the bag hold its shape. It also serves as the inner lining of the bag.

MATERIALS:

1 old tablecloth, or 1 yard home decor- or upholstery-weight fabric

1 yard cotton canvas

Sewing machine needles for heavy-weight sewing (I used size $100/16$)

Assorted seed and bugle beads

From the Crafter's Toolkit:

Iron and ironing board

Fabric scissors

Quilter's clear ruler

Rotary cutter and self-healing cutting mat

Sewing machine and coordinating thread

FriXion pen or water-soluble fabric marker

Straight pins

Small to medium-size paintbrush

Strong fabric glue (I used Aleen's Super Fabric Adhesive)

TO MAKE:

1) **Wash, dry, and press the tablecloth.** Don't prewash the canvas; its stiffness is helpful as you sew.

2) **Cut the fabric and lining.** Before you cut, decide what part of the fabric pattern you will want to add beads to, then cut the fabric so that area will not end up in a side seam.

   From the tablecloth, cut one piece for the main body, measuring 39 x 15 inches. For the bag's sides, cut two pieces measuring 17½ x 4 inches each. For the bag's straps, cut two pieces measuring 28 x 4¼ inches.

   From the canvas, cut one piece of lining for the main body, measuring 39 x 15 inches. Cut two pieces measuring 17½ x 4 inches each, to line the sides.

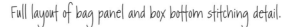

Full layout of bag panel and box bottom stitching detail.

3) **Make the straps.** Fold the strap pieces in half lengthwise, wrong sides together, and press. Next, open up the piece and fold the cut lengthwise edges toward the wrong side, so their edges meet at the middle crease, and press. Lastly, fold the strap lengthwise in half again to encase the folded edges, and press flat. Machine-stitch close to the edge on both lengthwise edges of each strap, using coordinating thread. It can be tricky to edge-stitch handles, so take your time and "walk" the straps through the machine if needed. (Note: The raw edges on each of the short ends will be encased in the bag when it's all sewn together.)

4) **Construct the main body of bag.** Mark the box bottom of the tote bag by first laying both the main and lining fabrics on your work surface with wrong sides together and the main outer fabric on top. On the outer fabric's right side, measure 17½ inches from one short edge, and using the FriXion pen or a water-soluble fabric marker and a ruler, draw a line at this measurement across the width. Repeat on the opposite side. Fold and press the two layers of fabric (main fabric and lining) at those lines, pinning the fold if needed. Machine stitch ¼ inch away from the folds, creating the box bottom of the bag (see illustration).

5) **Hem the opening and attach the handles to the tote.** At the opening of the tote, turn ½ inch of each layer toward its wrong side and press, repeat on other side. Next, measure across the top, 3½ inches in from each of the outer edges toward the middle, and mark with the FriXion or water-soluble marker; repeat on other side. Insert 1½ inches of one strap's short edge between the main and lining fabric layers, centered at each of these marks, and pin, making sure the handles are even and not twisted; do the same on the other side. Sew a ¼-inch topstitch across these edges, catching the handles in the seam as you go.

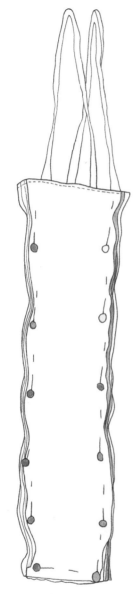

Pin side panels to body so edges
are exposed to the outside.

6) **Construct the sides of the bag.**
Lay a main body side piece and
lining side piece on top of each
other, wrong sides together. Turn
each fabric down ½ inch on one
of the short sides and press. Pin
these layers together, and sew
a ¼-inch seam across this short
side to create the hemmed top
edges of the tote. Repeat with
second set of side panels.

With one completed side
panel piece and plenty of pins, fit
and pin it into the side of the bag
body panels, lining up the top
hemmed edges evenly, keeping
the raw edges exposed on the
outside of the bag on the other
three sides *(see illustration)*.
The piecing and pinning for this
step can be fussy, but take your
time, and you'll get it. Repeat on
the other side of the bag. Sew
a generous ¼-inch seam on the
two sides and bottom of the bag.
You will see that this creates a
"box" effect at the bottom of
the bag. Trim the side seams to
even up and neaten, if necessary.
A little fraying of the edges will
occur; this is an intended part of
the look.

7) **Bead your tote.** With a FriXion
or water-soluble marking pen,
draw a light line to define what
area you will bead. I chose to
bead one area heavily and drew
sort of a comic strip "splat"
shape, but the possibilities for this
type of sparkle are vast. Spread
the glue well over one color area,
and then spread the beads in that
area. Work on beading one color
at a time if you are mimicking the
pattern in the fabric, and allow
that area to dry before moving
to the next. Beware: this step
is addictive, and you may find
yourself beading more than you
planned to. Once all the glue is
dry, you're done.

Glass Fishing Floats

I have long loved the simple, modern look of glass fishing floats. First produced by the Norwegians in the 1800s for fishermen to attach to their large fishing nets, they would bobble at the surface of the water, allowing the men to keep track of where their nets were. My nonutilitarian crocheted version will not be of much use to an actual fisherman; however, several of them hung together do make quite a beautiful art installation. The glass shimmers beautifully in sunlight or candlelight (they would also make pretty amazing holiday ornaments). You will need a bit of crochet experience to make these because of the size of the hook and the thread you will use, but the stitches themselves are basic. Essentially a mesh pattern, done in the round, from the bottom up. One skein of the perle cotton thread will cover several glass balls.

Note: Tension is not critical, but the crochet work should hold the glass ball securely. If you use balls of different sizes, adjust your increase and decrease rows accordingly to fit.

MATERIALS:

1 skein size 5 perle cotton thread (I used DMC)

Crochet hook, 2 mm (US size 4)

Locking stitch marker

Clear round ornaments (I used both clear and frosted 4-inch glass balls)

Note: Remove the metal top of the ornament, if it has one. You won't need it for this project.

From the Crafter's Toolkit:

All-purpose scissors

Abbreviations Used:

CH–chain stitch

SC–single crochet

SL ST–slip stitch

TO MAKE:

CH 6 and **SL ST** into the first **CH** to form a ring.

Round 1: **CH** 1, **SC** 12 into the center of the ring, **SL ST** into the first **SC** to join. Place a locking stitch marker to mark the beginning of the round.

Round 2: ***CH** 3, **SC** into the second **CH**, repeat from * to form six "loops" spaced evenly around your circle. **SL ST** into the beginning **CH** to join. (6 loops)

Round 3: ***CH** 4, sc into the **CH**-3 space from the previous round*. Repeat from * to * all the way around. **SL ST** into the beginning **CH** to join. (6 loops)

Round 4: **CH** 6, **SC** into the **CH**-4 space from the previous round*, repeat from * to * all the way around. **SL ST** into the beginning **CH** to join. (6 loops)

Round 5: **CH** 8, sc into the **CH**-6 space from the previous round*, repeat from * to * all the way around. **SL ST** into the beginning **CH** to join. (6 loops)

Round 6: **CH** 10, **SC** into the **CH**-8 space from the previous round*, repeat from * to * all the way around. **SL ST** into the beginning **CH** to join. (6 loops)

Rounds 7 and 8: **CH** 12, **SC** into the loop space from the previous round*, repeat from * to * all the way around. **SL ST** into the beginning **CH** to join. (6 loops)

Round 9: **CH** 8, **SC** into the **CH**-12 loop space from the previous round*, repeat from * to * all the way around. **SL ST** into the beginning **CH** to join. (6 loops)

At this point, slip the crocheted mesh over the ornament and finish the project on the ornament.

Round 10: **CH** 6, **SC** into the **CH**-8 loop space from the previous round*, repeat from * to * all the way around. **SL ST** into the beginning **CH** to join. (6 loops)

Round 11: **CH** 4, **SC** into the **CH**-6 loop space from the previous round*, repeat from * to * all the way around. **SL ST** into the beginning **CH** to join. (6 loops)

Round 12: **CH** 2, **SC** into the **CH**-4 loop space from the previous round*, repeat from * to * all the way around. **SL ST** into the beginning **CH** to join. (6 loops)

Once you get to the top of the ornament, create a chain of several inches to create a hanging "rope."

Hang several together at different lengths, tie the tails into one knot, and enjoy.

Summer Sherbet Picnic Blanket

Keep this in the car to have a substantial picnic blanket ready to spread out over damp grass and still keep bottoms nice and dry. The finished blanket is a 48-inch square made from an assortment of striped shirts (the brighter the better). By varying the colors and types of stripes in each shirt, the picnic blanket will have a vibrant feel.

MATERIALS:

10 striped woven dress shirts (you will need 10 squares from each shirt, so small shirts will work just fine)

1 machine-washable standard-size shower curtain liner

Small bulldog or binder clips

Yarn

½ yard 42- to 44-inch-wide solid quilting-weight fabric, for binding

From the Crafter's Toolkit:

Iron and ironing board

Fabric scissors

Quilter's clear ruler

Rotary cutter and self-healing cutting mat

Straight pins

Sewing machine and coordinating thread

Yarn needle with sharp tip

TO MAKE:

1) **Prepare the materials.** Wash, dry, and press the shirts. Remove the shower curtain liner from the packaging and lay it out flat or hang to allow wrinkles to fall out.

2) **Mark and cut squares from the shirts.** You will need to cut ten 5½-inch squares from each shirt (adjust the number of squares accordingly to make the blanket larger or smaller). Your stripes should always be straight vertically or horizontally, not diagonally. Consider using such details as the pockets and button plackets (you could put eating utensils in the pockets). You will need a total of one hundred squares, ten from each striped fabric.

3) **Lay out the design and construct the blanket top.** This is a variation of a traditional four-patch quilt pattern. On your work surface, lay out groups of four squares, each with two different stripe patterns, to create the square of four, using the photo and illustration as a guide for placement. I found it easiest to sew each group of four together, move on to the next group of four, and so on. All seams should be sewn with a ¼-inch seam allowance, and their seam allowances pressed open.

Sew the completed four-patch squares together, again using the illustration as a guide. Press open the seam allowances. The picnic blanket top is complete.

4) **Baste the blanket layers together.** On a flat surface, lay out the layers of the blanket as follows: shower curtain liner on the bottom, right side facing down (if there is one), and your completed blanket top on top, right side facing up. A bit of the liner (2 to 4 inches) should extend beyond

the quilt top on all four sides to ensure you will have enough; you'll trim the excess away later. Using as few pins as possible (pinholes will show permanently on the shower curtain liner), pin both layers together, starting in the center and working outward, smoothing the layers flat as you go. It can be fussy to pin through the shower curtain liner; take your time. Once you reach the edges, use bulldog clips to hold the layers together.

5) **Tie the layers together.** Using a hand-sewing yarn needle and yarn, working from the front of the blanket, and starting at the center of the blanket top and working outward, sew a short diagonal line in the middle of each four-patch set. Tie a square double knot on the front to secure and trim the tails to 3 inches. *(See illustration, page 91.)*

6) **Make and sew on the binding.** For this blanket, you'll need a total of 192 inches of binding (the total measurement of all four sides, plus 10 inches). Measure and cut 2½-inch-wide strips across the width of the solid-color fabric. Sew the strips together end to end at a 90-degree angle, right sides together, until all are joined into one continuous strip. Once joined, fold and press the entire strip in half lengthwise, wrong sides together. Unfold one of the short edges of the binding, trim it at a 45-degree angle, fold ¼

inch of the cut edge to the wrong side, press, and refold. This will be the end you will begin at when sewing onto your blanket.

Trim the edges of the blanket layers flush on all four sides, using a rotary cutter. Due to the thickness of the shower curtain liner fabric, you will machine-stitch the binding to the back of the blanket first, then fold over to the front and hand stitch. To attach the binding, start in the middle of one side of the blanket, and leave about 8 inches of the binding unsewn. With the raw edges of the binding aligned with the raw edge of the blanket, begin sewing the binding onto the liner side, using a ⅜-inch seam allowance. Continue until you reach a corner. To create a mitered corner, stop ¼ inch from the edge and secure with a backstitch. Remove from under the presser foot. Next, fold the loose binding up and away from the blanket's corner at a 45-degree angle, but then fold it

back down again, lining it up the raw edges with the edge of the blanket again. This creates the mitered fold. Turn the blanket 90 degrees and position the edge back under the machine, aligned to begin sewing the next side. Begin stitching ¼ inch from the fold you just made and continue along. Do this step for each corner.

When you are about 6 inches from where you began, stop sewing, backstitch to secure, and remove from under the presser foot. Position this binding edge neatly inside the beginning binding edge, trimming away any excess. Pin in place, if necessary, and continue sewing until the binding is completely attached.

Hand stitch binding to the front of the blanket, using small hemstitches.

CHAPTER THREE

FALL

I have an affection for those transitional seasons, the way they take the edge off the intense cold of winter or heat of summer.

— WHITNEY OTTO, *HOW TO MAKE AN AMERICAN QUILT*

I am a homebody and a nester by nature, and fall kicks these tendencies into full gear. Favorite sweaters come out, my children head back to school, and our new daily rhythm begins. I bring nature indoors with pots of moss and green leafy plants and change things up to make the house feel cozy. Quilts are thrown over couches (and sometimes bickered over). Fires are lit. Tea is made. We enjoy the season to the fullest.

Spooky Silhouettes p.99

Bat Photo Backdrop p.100

Spooky Dishes p.102

Sinister Ceramics p.105

Mummy-Wrapped Vases
and Votives p.106

Forest Walk Tabletop Garden p.109

Zombie Barbies p.110

Sweater Lampshade p.113

Aspen Branch Hooks p.114

Dip-Dyed Toile Dishes p.117

Faux Taxidermy p.118

Modern Crocheted Doily p.121

Tagged Toile Memo Board p.122

Gathering Bunting p.125

Faux Bois Quilt p.129

Spooky Silhouettes

This is my favorite type of Halloween decor: easy, subtle, and a little bit ominous. It begs a double take. I replace several pictures on our walls with these framed silhouettes for the month of October. Spruce up a set of old frames and print out the provided silhouettes or make some of your own.

MATERIALS:

Wooden picture frames

Black matte spray paint

Printer

Digital camera (or use silhouette templates, pages 176-177)

Matte-finish photo paper

Black scrapbooking paper (optional)

From the Crafter's Toolkit:

All-purpose cleaner and cloth

Painter's blue tape

Newspaper or drop cloth to protect work surface

Rubber gloves

Face mask

Apron

Fat and fine-point black permanent markers

Paper scissors

All purpose glue

TO MAKE:

1) **Prep the frames.** Clean the frames, and tape off any areas you don't want to paint. Lay down newspaper or a drop cloth to protect your work surface. Don the rubber gloves, face mask, and apron. Give the frames a few light coats of black spray paint and allow to dry.

2) **Create the silhouette images.** If making your own family silhouettes, take profile snapshots of everyone and print out to the desired size on matte photo paper. Color the faces and hair in completely with black permanent marker, and add your own sinister details, such as devil horns and witch's hats. Cut out the finished silhouettes.

   If desired, after cutting out the silhouettes, you can trace them onto solid black scrapbooking paper, using a black fine-point pen, then cut them out. Or you can simply photocopy the silhouette templates on page 176 and 177 in your desired size onto matte photo paper.

3) **Mount and frame your images.** If using your own images, glue each onto a clean piece of matte photo paper. Trim the photos to the desired size, insert into the picture frames, and hang.

OTHER IDEA:

* Think beyond Halloween for this project. Make bright birthday silhouettes with party hats or graduation silhouettes with caps.

Bat Photo Backdrop

Hang this at a Halloween party with a camera nearby and watch everyone have fun taking photos in front of it.

MATERIALS:

1 twin- or full-size white bedsheet

Simple image of a bat

Computer

Scanner (optional)

Printer

Card stock–weight paper

Black spray paint

From the Crafter's Toolkit:

Iron and ironing board

Craft knife

Self-healing cutting mat

Face mask

Rubber gloves

Apron

TO MAKE:

1) **Wash and iron the bedsheet.**

2) **Prepare the bat template.** Find an image of a bat online or in a science book. Adjust the size, if necessary, and use your computer or scanner, if needed, to print out onto white card stock–weight paper. On a self-healing cutting mat, cut around the black bat image with a craft knife. Keep the outline of the bat whole, as you'll use it as a painting template.

3) **Paint the bedsheet.** Lay out the bedsheet flat on a large area (I used my driveway). Don the face mask, rubber gloves, and apron. Place the template on the sheet and use black spray paint to fill. Move the template around the sheet, positioning the bats at different angles and continuing to fill the sheet. Allow to dry.

4) **Hang.** Tape the sheet onto a wall to use as a photo backdrop.

OTHER IDEA:

*   Use a photo backdrop like this for any kind of party. Try painting silver stars, colorful flowers or birds, or freehand paint words across a sheet.

Spooky Dishes

I wanted to use old medical diagrams around the house for Halloween one year, and that's where this project began. Look for fussy, old-fashioned, floral dishes with some white space in the design to add the decals and hang them on the wall (they won't be suitable for food after the decals are added).

MATERIALS:

Ceramic plates, jars, or teapots with old-fashioned floral motifs

Rubbing alcohol and cotton balls

Images to transfer (my images came from *Heck's Pictorial Archive of Nature and Science,* a copyright-free Dover clip art book)

Computer

Scanner (optional)

Printer

Waterslide decal transfer paper (I used Lazertran)

Bowl of warm water

Sponge

From the Crafter's Toolkit:

Small scissors

Sponge brush

Craft glue (I used Mod Podge)

TO MAKE:

1) **Wash and dry the dishes.** Rubbing the surface with an alcohol-dipped cotton ball will remove fingerprints.

2) **Create the transfer images.** Decide what you will create decals of and scan them into your computer, resizing them if necessary. Print out the images onto the waterslide decal paper, following the package instructions. Fit as many images as you can onto one 8½ x 11-inch sheet, then trim around them, to avoid waste. Allow for drying time, if needed.

3) **Cut out the images.** Using small scissors, cut around your images. Leave a scant ¼-inch margin all around each image.

4) **Apply the images to the dishes.** Immerse your first decal in a bowl of warm water until the white paper backing starts to release from the decal. Slip the decal carefully off the backing paper and apply right side up to the dish. Carefully smooth out any wrinkles with a clean, damp sponge and allow to dry thoroughly.

5) **Seal the image.** Using a sponge brush and a coat of craft glue, seal your dishes. Read your decal paper package instructions for any special instructions.

Sinister Ceramics

There is no shortage of ceramic kitty, owl, and bird curios at the thrift store. Although they may not look so appealing just sitting there on the shelf together, they make great Halloween decorations with just a little paint. In fact, it's hard to put them away after Halloween. My daughter Emma kept an eagle she named Vulture on her desk for over a year.

MATERIALS:

Ceramic figurines (e.g., owls, cats, or birds)

Soap and water

Black matte spray paint

Red flat-back or adhesive-back jewels

From the Crafter's Toolkit:

Newspaper or drop cloth to protect work surface

Face mask

Rubber gloves

Apron

Craft glue

TO MAKE:

1) **Clean your figurines.** Wash in warm, soapy water and allow to dry.

2) **Paint the pieces.** Lay down newspaper or a drop cloth to protect your work surface. Don the face mask, rubber gloves, and apron. Give the figurines a few light coats of black spray paint and allow to dry.

3) **Embellish them even more.** Apply jewels to their eyes, using craft glue, if needed.

OTHER IDEAS:

* Turn lovebird figurines into Valentine's Day pieces with red or pink paint.

* Cluster a brightly colored set on a summer party table.

Mummy-Wrapped Vases and Votives

A simple, pretty effect for the Halloween season. Get the kids to help with the wrapping and stitching of the cheesecloth.

MATERIALS:

Assorted clear glass vases and votive holders

Cheesecloth (at least 4 feet)

Battery-operated tea lights

From the Crafter's Toolkit:

Fabric scissors

Black sewing thread

Hand-sewing needle

TO MAKE:

1) **Cut the cheesecloth.** Cut several wide, short strips that will each wrap once around a vase.

2) **Wrap the vase.** Wrap several of the strips around the glass vase, having all the short edges meet on one side of the vase when wrapping.

3) **Stitch.** To stitch and secure the cheesecloth, hand sew with a needle and black thread. Sew stitches up the side of the vase in a wavy line, knotting them each individually to look like sutures.

4) **Add the lights.** Add battery-operated tea lights in each vase or votive (larger vases can hold several) and enjoy the glow. (Regular candles might make this project a little more exciting than you'd want!)

Forest Walk Tabletop Garden

Fall is lively, gorgeous, and short-lived. Let's get the family out there to enjoy it. There is an actual enchanted forest just a short walk from our house (well, okay, we think it's enchanted). Each walk produces yet another new collection of little bits of nature. Create bowl gardens like this, using these found pieces. This is the type of project I love. It combines memories of good times with my family with useful living things, such as plants, which helps to purify stuffy indoor air when the house is shut up in the cold weather months.

MATERIALS:

Vessel or bowl

Soap and water

Pea gravel or small pebbles

Potting mix

Succulent plants in various shades of green

Found and foraged bits of nature:

> *Dried hydrangea heads*
>
> *Seedpods*
>
> *Driftwood*
>
> *Smooth rocks or ones covered with moss*
>
> *Twigs covered in lichen*
>
> *Pinecones*
>
> *Evergreen branches*
>
> *Fall leaves, for temporary but vibrant color*

Spray bottle filled with water

TO MAKE:

1) **Prepare the planting container.** Wash and dry the vessel thoroughly. Add a layer of pebbles, ¼ to ½ inch, for drainage in the bottom of the vessel.

2) **Arrange the succulent plants.** Think in groups of three, and spread the color variations around in the planter. Once you've placed these as you think you want them, plant them with potting mix.

3) **Layer in your found objects.** Place them all around the plant bases, covering the soil and adding color and texture all over the planter.

4) **Water the plants.** Give the entire planter a thorough spraying with water to clean off the plants and pack down the surface of the soil. Place where it gets bright indirect light throughout much of the day and allow to dry between watering ("loving neglect," as I like to call it).

Zombie Barbies

There is a pile of naked Barbies in the toy section of any thrift store, just waiting for this project. A group of these ladies will create instant Halloween party smiles.

MATERIALS:

Barbie dolls

Soap and water

White spray paint

Doll stands (optional; available at craft and hobby stores)

From the Crafter's Toolkit:

Fine-point black marker

Newspaper or drop cloth to protect work surface

Face mask

Rubber gloves

Apron

TO MAKE:

1) **Clean the dolls.** Wipe them well with soap and water, and allow to dry.

2) **Paint the pieces.** Spread newspaper or a drop cloth to protect your work surface. Don the face mask, rubber gloves, and apron. Give each Barbie several coats of white spray paint and allow to dry. Cover their hair, eyes, everything. (The hair may melt a little, but that's all part of the "charm.")

3) **Add small details.** Add details to the eyes and mouth, using a fine-point black marker. Perhaps they need tattoos?

4) **Display.** Stand up each doll on a doll stand, if desired, in a group, with arms pointed forward.

Sweater Lampshade

With my love of all things cozy, it's no wonder that unexpected things get wrapped in layers around our house when the temperature dips. I've wrapped votive holders, computers, and now lamps. Inspired by the small and rustic cabin I hope to have some day (for now, it lives in my head), I gave this lamp a coat of paint and a Fair Isle sweater shade. It's strikingly simple, with contrasting hand stitches that only add to the character.

MATERIALS:

Old lamp and sturdy wire shade (the lamp shade I used is smaller at the top, and worked great for a more fitted sweater)

Spray paint

1 Fair Isle sweater (moth holes are totally acceptable for this project, but check the size of the sweater against your lampshade: I used a women's size small)

Medium-size to large bulldog or binder clips

Scrap yarn in coordinating but contrasting colors

From the Crafter's Toolkit:

All-purpose cleaner and cloth

Painter's blue tape

Newspaper or drop cloth to protect work surface

Face mask

Rubber gloves

Fabric scissors

Apron

Yarn needle

TO MAKE:

1) **Prepare the lamp base for painting.** Remove the lampshade, and clean and dry the lamp base. Cover the cord and any parts of the lamp base you don't plan to paint with tape. Lay down newspaper or a drop cloth to protect your work surface. Don the face mask, rubber gloves, and apron. Spray three to four light coats of spray paint over the lamp base and allow to dry.

2) **Recover the lampshade.** Pull the old fabric off the lampshade, leaving just the wire shade base. Pull the sweater over the shade, from the top (the neck will be at the top of the shade). Cut off the arms, including the armhole seams (this will leave openings, which you will sew closed). Fold the top edge of the sweater over the top edge of the shade and clip with bulldog clip to hold in place. Do the same at the bottom. Trim away any excess.

3) **Sew up holes in the sweater.** Pull each opening snugly to the shade, and sew closed, using a yarn needle and yarn (color can be contrast or matching). The stitches you make will show (which is the point), so go slow to keep them uniform. Begin at the bottom of the opening and tie a knot on the inside. Trim away excess sweater knit as necessary to create a snug fit.

4) **Sew the top and bottom edges of the sweater to the shade.** With contrast yarn, sew large stitches around the top and bottom edges of the lampshade, encasing the sweater around the wire. Trim away the extra sweater fabric carefully from the inside of the shade. I loved the way the yarn tails looked at the bottom of the shade and decided to leave a few hanging and visible. I also left intact the small pocket on my sweater, which is now part of the shade.

5) **Cozy up!** Put the shade on the lamp, and find the perfect spot to place it in your imaginary cabin (preferable close to a cup of tea, a quilt, and a good book).

Aspen Branch Hooks

These surprisingly sturdy wall hooks bring a little nature into the house, and I love that we can make them ourselves. Ours hold everything from school bags to my overabundance of necklaces. We gathered fallen branches while walking through my in-laws' property in Colorado, which make these a nice reminder of that day.

MATERIALS:

Aspen or some other type of strong wood branch with suitable joints to be used as hooks

Saw

Drill

Gloss-finish spray paint

2 screws

From the Crafter's Toolkit:

Ruler

Sandpaper

Newspaper or drop cloth to protect work surface

Face mask

Rubber gloves

Apron

TO MAKE:

1) **Cut the branch joint.** Mine measure about 6 inches long.

2) **Cut away the back of the branch joint.** Flatten the back of the branch that will be against the wall by sawing or sanding it down. If needed, sand the rest of the branch to smooth any rough edges.

3) **Drill two holes through the branch,** one at the top and one at the bottom, each about ½ inch from each edge.

4) **Paint the hook.** Lay down newspaper or a drop cloth to protect your work surface. Don the face mask, rubber gloves, and apron. Spray the branch with several light coats of spray paint to finish and allow to dry.

5) **Hang.** Attach to the wall securely with two screws.

OTHER IDEA:

* I'd love to see these in neon colors. Maybe even glittered and varnished over. Now that would be really fun!

Dip-Dyed Toile Dishes

Maybe you've found yourself the recipient of family dishes that you secretly wish looked a little more you, or maybe you've come across beautiful toile dishes at the thrift store (like I did) and just want to have some fun. By adding a few brush strokes of ceramic paint, then baking according to the manufacturer's directions, you can add a simple and modern twist to fussy-looking patterned china. I made these pieces using transparent, harvest-inspired colors for our Thanksgiving table, and we now use these dishes all the time. I did an entire set of dishes in one afternoon.

MATERIALS:

Oven

Ceramic dishes

Rubbing alcohol and cotton balls

Pebeo Porcelaine 150 ceramic paint in your choice of colors (I used Peridot Green 30, Coral Red 05, and Amber Brown 36)

Paper plate

Water

From the Crafter's Toolkit:

Paper towels or cloth

Wide paintbrush

TO MAKE:

1) **Prepare the dishes.** Preheat your oven to 350°F. Wash and dry all the pieces you plan to paint. Rubbing the surface with an alcohol-dipped cotton ball will remove fingerprints.

2) **Prepare the paint.** Pour a small amount of the Pebeo Porcelaine 150 ceramic paint onto a paper plate. Add a few drops of water to thin it out only slightly. Try to avoid creating bubbles by stirring lightly and slowly.

3) **Paint the dishes.** Using your paintbrush, swipe a thin layer of the ceramic paint over half (or less) of the plate, to create the look of "dipping" the plate into a bucket of dye. I intentionally kept the effect transparent to let the pattern show through.

4) **Bake the dishes.** Once you've painted all the pieces, carefully place them directly on the racks in your oven and let them bake for 30 minutes. When the baking is complete, turn off the oven but leave the pieces in the oven for a few hours to allow them to cool down gradually.

OTHER IDEAS:

* Add gold or silver accents around the rims and handles with ceramic paint pens (but keep in mind that they shouldn't go in the microwave afterward).

* Try this idea on mismatched flatware: Dip the handles and bake as directed.

Faux Taxidermy

This project is a gentler, kinder form of taxidermy, using faux-feathered birds from my local craft store's floral section instead of the real thing. I intentionally used a minimum amount colors and kept the backgrounds spare, to give these a modern feel. Their labels were made on the computer.

MATERIALS:

Shadowbox frames that will hold birds comfortably (I used both 5 x 7- and 8 x 10-inch frames with an inside depth of about 1³/₄ inches)

1 sheet ³/₁₆-inch thick (or thinner) sheet of white foam core board

1 (⁷/₁₆-inch diameter) wooden dowel

Saw or heavy knife

Thumbtack with flat top

Spray paint (I used Primer Gray)

Craft store birds (simple or fantastical; you decide)

Small scraps of fake moss

Computer

Printer

All-purpose printer paper

Scrap fabric

Picture-hanging hardware (optional)

From the Crafter's Toolkit:

Pencil

Craft knife

Ruler

Self-healing cutting mat

Painter's blue tape

Sandpaper

Newspaper or drop cloth to protect work surface

Face mask

Rubber gloves

Apron

All-purpose scissors

Hot glue gun

Craft glue (I used Mod Podge)

TO MAKE:

1) **Cut a new back for the frame and prepare it for painting.** Remove the back of the shadowbox frame; we won't be using it. Trace this shape onto the sheet of foam core board. Cut out, using a craft knife and a ruler, on a self-healing cutting mat. Either remove the glass from the frame or tape it off both inside and outside, using painter's blue tape.

2) **Cut a perch for the bird.** Cut a 1-inch-long piece of dowel and sand the ends smooth. Stick a flat thumbtack through one end and stand the dowel completely upright to paint it.

3) **Paint the pieces.** Lay down newspaper or drop cloth to protect your work surface. Don the face mask, rubber gloves, and apron. Spray-paint the inside and outside of the frames, the foam core board (one side only), and the wooden perch. Allow to dry.

4) **Position the perch.** Think about how and where the bird will be positioned in the frame. Will the frame hang portrait or landscape? Using a glue gun, glue one end of the perch to the painted side of the foam core board, positioning it slightly below center, to allow room for the bird on top.

5) **Add the bird.** Clip off any wire or feet and hot glue the bird to the perch. Glue a small clump of moss to the dowel around where the bird sits.

6) **Create the labels.** On the computer, type out a label. (The Latin names of my birds were completely made up, which was fun to do.) Play around with different fonts until you find one you like; italic or script looks more handwritten. Print and cut out the labels.

   Cut out a scrap of fabric slightly larger than the label, so it will show behind it. Use craft glue to first glue the label to the backing fabric, then glue the label to be centered under the bird.

7) **Assemble the shadowbox and hang.** Insert the finished foam core backing into the frame, attach picture-framing hardware, if needed, and hang.

Modern Crocheted Doily

Fall arrives, and with it comes all kinds of after-school activities. For me, this can mean plenty of sitting, watching, and waiting. Idle hands are lost crafting opportunities, so I always have something portable and quick with me to pass the time. One ball of yarn and one hook is all you need to make these crocheted disks. Once I had a bagful, I sewed them together and made them into a table runner for our dining room table, but there are a hundred different ways to use these little disks: a scarf, a string of bunting, or to top off a package. And if you have to do a lot of waiting, maybe you'll even have enough for an afghan!

Note: Gauge is not critical for this project, as long as the disks are roughly the same size.

MATERIALS:

Several colors of yarn (leftover yarn from previous projects is perfect, but if you are buying yarn, choose a worsted weight. My favorite is Cascade 220 100% wool.)

Crochet hook, 4.0 mm (US size G)

From the Crafter's Toolkit:

Yarn needle

scissors

Abbreviations Used:

CH—chain stitch

DC—double crochet

SC—single crochet

SL ST—slip stitch

TO MAKE:

To crochet one disk:

CH 2, **SC** 6 times into the beginning **CH**, **SL ST** into the first **SC** to join into a circle.

Round 1: **CH** 1, 1 **SC** in the same stitch, 2 **SC** in each **SC** around, **SL ST** to join the last stitch with the first stitch. (12 sts)

Round 2: **CH** 3, **DC** 1 into the first **SC** from the previous round (equals 2 **DC**), then **DC** 2 into each **SC** all the way around, **SL ST** into the third **CH** from the beginning to join. (24 sts)

To sew the disks together:

Using contrasting yarn and a yarn needle, sew a stitch or two, as shown in the photo, to attach the disks.

Tagged Toile Memo Board

We have to get ourselves organized in the fall. School forms, sports physicals, and new schedules all need a place to be seen and remembered. I came up with this board to hang on the wall near where we come and go. It's now the place to look for any important form that Mom was supposed to sign. Toile has always been one of my favorite fabrics, but it has always felt too fussy for us. But I can't leave things alone, so I captioned the lovely pastoral scenes on an old toile tablecloth with things more in keeping with the dry humor heard around here. I call it "tagging" because it felt like I was doing some embroidered graffiti. Fun to design and another portable project!

MATERIALS:

½ yard toile fabric (larger prints are easier to embroider)

4 or 5 colors of embroidery thread (I used DMC)

Unframed corkboard (the one I used is 17 x 23 inches)

Staple gun and staples

Picture-hanging hardware (optional)

From the Crafter's Toolkit:

Iron and ironing board

FriXion pen or water-soluble fabric marker

Embroidery hoop

All-purpose scissors

Embroidery needle

Quilter's clear ruler

Rotary cutter and self-healing cutting mat

Sewing machine and coordinating thread (optional)

TO MAKE:

1) **Prepare the toile fabric to embroider.** If necessary, wash and iron the fabric. Then get inspired by the funny things that are said and done in your family. Using a FriXion pen or water-soluble marker, write what you wish to embroider directly onto the right side of the toile. To create patchwork squares like mine, concentrate the design of your embroidery within a 5-inch-square area of the print, which you will then cut around to create one patchwork square. Keep in mind the finished size of your board: You will want to embroider enough of the toile to completely cover the front of the board.

3) **Cut the toile into patchwork squares (optional).** If you like, cut each of the toile scenes into 5½-inch squares. Join the squares together in a patchwork manner, machine sewing all seams with a ¼-inch seam allowance. Press the seam allowances open.

4) **Cover the front of the cork-board.** Lay the fabric, right side up, over the front of the cork board, pulling the fabric snugly around to the back. Staple in place on the back and trim any excess fabric.

5) **Attach picture-hanging hardware, if needed, and hang.**

OTHER IDEAS:

* Add other embellishments to the scenes such as sequins or beads.

* Use fabric paint to add more color.

2) **Embroider the toile.** Embroidery floss has six strands. Separate it into two sets of three strands, and embroider with a length of three strands at a time. Fit the area of the fabric you will stitch into an embroidery hoop to help you keep even tension. Begin embroidering the toile, using a simple backstitch, following the lines and words you drew. To create a backstitch, first make a single stitch along your line. Next, insert the needle up through the back, ¼ inch away from the first stitch, still following your line, then insert the needle back into the hole of the previous stitch. Continue in this manner to stitch over all the letters and words.

Also fill in random areas, such as leaves on the trees and other details. Think of other things to add. Should the lady wear a "peace" necklace with her ball gown? Why not?

Gathering Bunting

The joke is that it's "on the family DVD" when we start retelling family antics, but honestly, we love a good story. Without extended family nearby, I created this bunting filled with photos of important people in our life. It helps kids understand their family history and remember they are part of something bigger. By using printable canvas sheets, you create a bunting durable enough to withstand years of parties, table gatherings, and family stories.

MATERIALS:

Family photos (I used 10, but left room on the ends for more)

Computer and basic photo-editing software

Scanner (optional)

Printer

Printable canvas sheets (I used Strathmore Artist Inkjet Papers)

Saucer or bowl

5/16-inch white nylon cord

Felt and fabric remnants in your choice of colors

From the Crafter's Toolkit:

Fine-point pen

All-purpose scissors

Ruler

Fabric scissors

Hot glue gun

TO MAKE:

1) **Gather your photos.** If they are not already in your computer, you will need to scan them in. Size them to be about 4 x 6 inches, which will allow you to print two photos per canvas sheet and minimize waste. Print out on the canvas paper according to the package instructions. Cut out each individual photo, leaving no border.

2) **Create a curved edge on the bottom of the photos.** On the back of the photo, trace around a saucer or bowl, then cut.

3) **Make fabric flowers.** Use the same materials and method in the Recycled Floral Mirror project (page 35).

4) **Create the bunting.** Measure out a length of nylon cord (for ten photos, I cut a length of about 100 inches, leaving extra so more photos could be added later). Using a hot glue gun, begin adding the photos to the cord, applying a thin line of glue across the top back of each photo. The photos should just touch at the top corners, all the way across the cord. Once the photos are glued on, begin gluing the flowers to the cord. Cluster them in between each of the photos.

Hang and let the family stories begin.

OTHER IDEA:

* This would be so sweet for a child's birthday party. Add photos for every year of life, and use small trinkets or toys in place of the flowers.

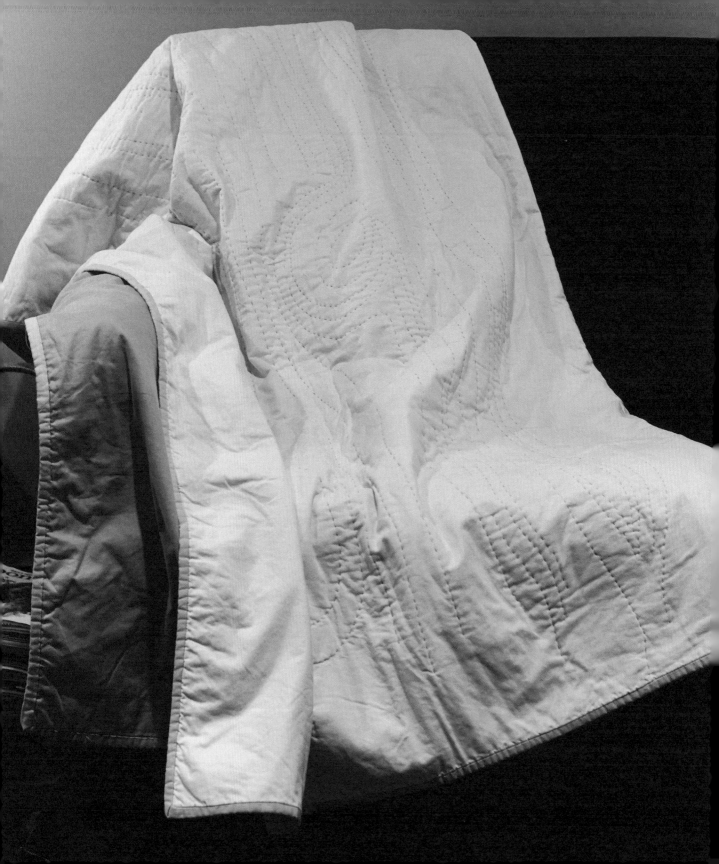

Faux Bois Quilt

I like quilts that are not overtly feminine or masculine, which is exactly how this one feels to me. The simple, understated beauty of faux bois (French for "false wood") really lends itself to hand stitching, so it felt right to make the stitches the star of the quilt. A whole-cloth quilt is a simple construction, very doable for all skill levels, with no fussy piecing or patchwork. By using a repurposed cotton bedsheet for both the front and back of the quilt, it's a very low-cost project. Relax into the hand stitching on a project like this one; it's worth taking advantage of the opportunity to slow down and enjoy the process. The finished size is 80 x 67 inches.

MATERIALS:

2 full- or queen-size solid-color flat cotton bedsheets (I chose a mustard shade for one side, and yellow for the other)

¾ yard 42- to 44-inch-wide solid quilting weight fabric, for the binding (I used Kona Cotton #1007 Ash)

1 package queen-size quilt batting (I used Warm & Natural 100% cotton batting)

Quilting thread

Quilting hoop

1 skein of contrasting perle cotton thread in size 8

From the Crafter's Toolkit:

Iron and ironing board

Quilter's clear ruler

Rotary cutter and self-healing cutting mat

FriXion pen or water-soluble fabric marker

Painter's blue tape

Quilter's or regular safety pins

Hand-sewing quilting needle

Thimble

Fabric scissors

Size 9 crewel embroidery needle

Sewing machine and coordinating thread

TO MAKE:

1) **Wash the sheets and binding fabric thoroughly.** (Tip: I usually wash thrifted bedsheets three or four times before I use them.) Press everything well.

2) **Mark out the faux bois pattern.** Decide which of the sheets will be the front of the quilt and trim it to 81 x 68 inches, using a rotary cutter and self-healing cutting mat. Lay it out on a flat surface (e.g., a floor or dining room table) to mark the faux bois quilting lines with a FriXion or water-soluble marker. I found it easiest to freehand these, after Googling some images for "faux bois" to use as reference. Use the illustration as reference, page 130.

3) **Create the quilt sandwich and baste it together.** On your work surface, lay out the sheet to use as the back, right side down. (Don't cut the sheet yet.) Use painter's blue tape on all four sides to keep this layer flat and smooth. Lay the quilt batting over the backing layer (it should be approximately the same size as the backing sheet), smoothing it as you go. The last layer will be the front sheet, right side up. Center this sheet over the backing and batting layers. The backing sheet and quilt batting should extend out past the edges of the top layer on all four sides by at least a couple of inches, and that's good.

Start pinning the layers together from the center of the quilt top, using quilter's or regular safety pins. Work your way out in a grid pattern, pinning every 4 inches or so. Take time to do this step thoroughly, smoothing the layers out well. Once this step is completed, you can remove the tape and move the quilt.

4) **Hand quilt the faux bois pattern.** Using your hand-sewing quilting needle, thimble, and quilting thread, begin sewing the lines drawn on the top sheet, using a simple running stitch, keep your stitches uniform and as small as you can. As in the basting/pinning process, I always prefer to start in the center of the quilt and work outward, removing the safety pins as you stitch. Using a quilting hoop will help maintain more even tension.

When all the quilting lines are stitched, use a rotary cutter, quilter's clear ruler, and self-healing mat underneath, trim all the edges evenly to measure 80 x 67 inches.

5) **Create and sew on the binding.** Cut eight strips widthwise, selvedge to selvedge from your binding fabric, measuring 2½ inches wide each. Sew the strips together end to end at a 90-degree angle, right sides together, until all of them are joined into one continuous strip.

Fold and press the entire strip in half lengthwise, wrong sides together. Unfold one of the short edges of the binding, trim it at a 45-degree angle, fold ¼ inch of the cut edge to the wrong side, press, and refold. This will be the end you will begin at when sewing onto your quilt.

To attach the binding, start in the middle of one side of the quilt, and leave about 8 inches of the binding unsewn. With the raw edges of the binding aligned with the raw edge of the quilt, begin machine sewing the binding onto the front side, using a ⅜-inch seam allowance. Continue until you reach a corner. To create a mitered corner, stop ¼ inch from the edge and secure with a backstitch. Remove from under the presser foot. Next, fold the loose binding up and away from the quilt's edge at a 45-degree angle, but then fold it back down again, lining it up the raw edges with the edge

of the quilt again. This creates the mitered fold. Turn the quilt 90 degrees and position the edge back under the machine, aligned to begin sewing the next side. Begin stitching ¼ inch from the fold you just made and continue along. Do this step for each corner.

Fold binding over the edge and hand stitch to the back of the quilt, using small hemstitches.

6) **Wash your quilt.** If you marked your quilt top with a FriXion pen, iron over your quilt top before washing it (water-soluble ink will come out in the wash.)

CHAPTER FOUR

WINTER

Winter is the time for comfort,
for good food and warmth,
for the touch of a friendly hand
and for a talk beside the fire:
it is the time for home.

— EDITH SITWELL, *TAKEN CARE OF: AN AUTOBIOGRAPHY*

We handcrafters live for the holiday season, and I usually have long, ambitious lists of things to make, decorate, bake, and give this time of year. Home becomes a cozy refuge at the end of our busy days; tabletops are often filled with books, scented candles, and a vase of fresh flowers, leaving little room for anything more. Weekends are popcorn- and movie-filled afternoons. Heavier textiles, such as curtains, quilts, and rugs, fill the house and protect us from the cold that seems to seep in from every corner.

Upcycled Gift Jars p.137

Holiday Table Display p.138

Hottie Rice Pillow p.141

Fresh Flower Tree Decorations p.144

Hostess Flowers p.147

Whoville Holiday Tree Decorations p.148

Fabric Scrap Flower Brooch p.151

Leather Appliquéd Pillow p.152

Sewn Furniture p.155

Rain Boot Warmers p.156

Advent Calendar p.158

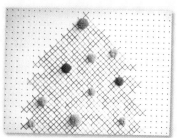

Giant Cross-Stitched Tree p.163

Handmade Checker Set p.164

Knitted Swatch Blanket p.167

Avalon Quilt p.170

Upcycled Gift Jars

Gifts in jars are always well received, especially when the jars can be used and reused well after the actual gift has been enjoyed. Think beyond food and fill them Legos, markers, or love notes. As a bonus, the small toys you add to the jar can be used to hang on the tree.

MATERIALS:

Pretty jars with tightly fitting lids

Soap and water

A small child's toy, such as a plastic animal

Small eye screw

Hammer (optional)

Glitter

Craft felt, scraps of ribbon

From the Crafter's Toolkit:

Newspaper to protect work surface

Paintbrush

Craft glue (I used Mod Podge)

All-purpose scissors

TO MAKE:

1) **Wash and dry the jars.**

2) **Glitter the toy.** Add a small eye screw to the toy to hang it with, tapping in with a hammer, if needed, to attach it securely. Spread newspaper to protect your work surface. Glitter the animal by painting, covering the surface with a coat of craft glue and sprinkling generously with glitter. Tap off the excess and allow to dry.

3) **Create a decorative tie.** Cut a length of craft felt, ½ to ¾ inch wide. With scissors, cut tiny little snips into each short end, to create the effect of fringe on a scarf. Thread the "scarf" through the eye screw on the toy, and tie around the neck of the jar. (Optionally, simply tie a length of ribbon.)

Holiday Table Display

I am not a big fan of cheap disposable party decorations. Instead, when we have a party, I go around the house and out in the yard, looking for things to decorate with or create without too much effort, and you know what? I always find something!

Napkins

MATERIALS:

Lightweight cotton fabric (think pretty floral sheets, outgrown Pinpoint Oxford men's shirts, etc.)

From the Crafter's Toolkit:

Iron and ironing board

Quilter's clear ruler

FriXion pen or water-soluble fabric marker

Fabric scissors

Sewing machine and coordinating thread

TO MAKE NAPKINS:

1) **Prewash and press the fabric.**

2) **Create the napkins.** Measure and mark a 15-inch line on the wrong side of the fabric, using a clear quilter's ruler and a FriXion pen or water-soluble fabric marker. Snip into the fabric at the edge of this line with fabric scissors, then tear. The fabric will tear on the straight of grain; don't worry if it doesn't tear straight across the drawn line. That's okay, but use the torn line as your new straight edge and measure the other sides from that. Repeat this step for the other three sides of the napkin: measure and mark the 15-inch line, snip the edge, and tear. Turn edges back a scant ½ inch two times, and hem with a straight stitch.

Place Card Holders

1) **Prepare the votive.** Clean the votive, then add a bit of clay or floral foam at the bottom. Cover this area with scraps of fake moss (hot glue this in if you want something a little more permanent.

2) **Prepare the labels.** Add washi tape or a bit of paper to one side of the bamboo skewer to make a flag. Write the name on the flag. Finish by poking the skewer down into the clay or floral foam.

MATERIALS:

Glass votives

Small bit of clay or floral foam (to hold skewers)

Small scraps of fake moss

Bamboo skewers

Washi tape or scraps of paper

From the Crafter's Toolkit:

All-purpose scissors

Fine-point black marker

Hot glue (optional)

Hottie Rice Pillow

Everybody in our house has at least one rice pillow like this, and I don't think we could get through our damp Seattle winters without them. Shaped as a traditional hot water bottle, these are the perfect size for warming toes or comforting upset tummies. The cover is removable for washing, and the rice can last for a long, long time. You can also use these in the summer, too. Just put them in the freezer and let them get very cold. Instant relief from the heat! The finished size is about 8 x 10 inches.

MATERIALS:

½ yard cotton flannel (a recycled flannel shirt is perfect for this project)

½ yard 100% cotton fabric, for lining (I repurposed a white cotton pillowcase)

Hottie Rice Pillow template (see page 179)

2 ¼ pounds uncooked rice

Funnel

From the Crafter's Toolkit:

Iron and ironing board

FriXion pen or water-soluble fabric marker

Pencil

Straight pins

All-purpose and fabric scissors

Sewing machine and coordinating thread

Quilter's clear ruler

Pinking shears (optional, for trimming raw edges)

TO MAKE:

1) **Prepare the fabric.** Prewash, dry, and press both the flannel and the lining fabric.

2) **Make the inner pillow.** Trace the provided Hottie Rice Pillow template onto a sheet of paper and cut it out. Trace the paper template twice onto the lining fabric, and cut out. Pin the lining pieces together with wrong sides facing, leaving the opening where indicated on template. Machine sew around the perimeter, using ¼-inch seam allowance. (Tip: It's helpful to use a smaller stitch to hold the rice in securely, so adjust your sewing machine stitch length accordingly.) Turn right sides out, pushing corners out fully and carefully.

   Using a funnel, fill the bag with about 2 ¼ pounds of uncooked rice. Once filled, machine stitch the opening closed, using a ¼-inch seam allowance. At this point, check to be sure the entire bag is sewn shut securely, and set aside as you make the cover.

3) **Make the outer cover panels.** Using the same paper template, trace it onto the wrong side of the flannel and cut out for the front side of the cover. The cover has an envelope back, so it can be easily removed and laundered. To make the back panels, first fold the paper pattern template in half lengthwise and crease. Now open it up and lay it on your fabric. Trace the bottom half of the template to the crease, then measuring and marking with a quilter's clear ruler and FriXion pen or water soluble marker, add 2 ½ inches beyond the crease line. Cut out. Repeat with the top half of the cover, also adding 2 ½ inches to the length.

   Hem the edges of the back cover panels that will be toward the middle of the pillow by turning back ¼ inch toward wrong

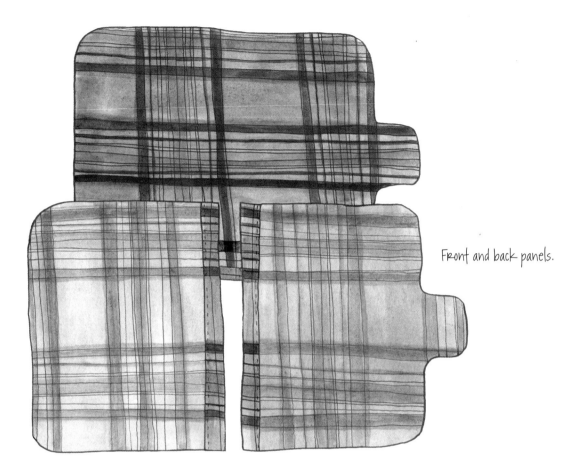

Front and back panels.

side, pressing, then turning back another ¼ inch to encase the raw edge, and pressing. Stitch across to create a hem, a scant ¼ inch from the folded edge. Repeat for both pieces of back outer cover (*see illustration*).

4) **Sew the outer cover panels together and finish.** On your work surface lay out the front cover, right side up; the top half of back cover, right side down; and bottom half of back cover,

right side down. The hemmed edges of the back cover panels should overlap at the middle. Pin around all sides and stitch, using a ¼-inch seam allowance. Clip the corners to ease bulk. Trim the seam allowance around the edges with pinking shears, if desired. Turn right side out, push the corners out, and press.

Insert your rice pillow into the cover.

To Use:

To heat in the microwave, start with 2 minutes at full power and adjust accordingly. Microwaves vary in wattage, so figure out the heating time that works best for yours. If giving as a gift, add instructions on how to heat and, if desired, sew in a loop for hanging up when not in use.

Fresh Flower Tree Decorations

I have always wanted to create a tree with just fresh flowers; it would feel like a little summer in the middle of winter. This idea would work beautifully as a last-minute decoration idea for a holiday tree or a small tabletop tree for a party, using a few inexpensive grocery store flower bouquets. Use flowers that won't wilt quickly, such as statice or carnations. Be sure to take pictures!

MATERIALS:

2 or 3 mixed floral bouquets from the supermarket

Floral tubes filled with water (optional, to preserve flowers longer)

Green pipe cleaners

Artificial or live evergreen tree

From the Crafter's Toolkit:

All-purpose scissors

TO MAKE:

1) **Create the floral bunches.** Cut the flower stems to a short length and make small mixed posies of flowers. Fill the floral tubes with water and add to the stems, if desired.

2) **Attach to the tree.** Twist a green pipe cleaner around the stems to hold them together. Twist the bunches and their pipe cleaners around the branches on the tree.

Hostess Flowers

My rule is to never come to anyone's house for a party empty-handed. This is a unique way to present flowers to the hostess. The straw box was a thrift store find. Not only is it an unexpected vessel for the flowers, it can be reused. I can't believe I didn't spray paint it first, but I liked the color of the straw.

MATERIALS:

Any unique container (e.g., interesting bowls, small vintage suitcases, oddly shaped baskets)

Plastic wrap

Floral foam roughly the size of your container

Serrated knife

Water

2 or 3 supermarket flower bouquets

Gift tag

From the Crafter's Toolkit:

Rubber gloves

All-purpose scissors

TO MAKE:

1) **Prepare the container.** Spread plastic wrap to cover the inside to hold in any moisture.

   If needed, cut the floral foam to size with a serrated knife. (Note: Always wear rubber gloves when handling floral foam; it contains formaldehyde.) Prepare it by soaking it in water for a few minutes before fitting it in the container.

2) **Add flowers.** Cut the flower stems short and poke them into the floral foam, creating your arrangement. The goal is to completely hide the floral foam and the edges of the container.

   Finish with a gift tag.

147

Whoville Holiday Trees

A few sweater and plaid wool scraps from my fabric stash yielded a bright little forest of trees for the winter mantle.

MATERIALS:

Wool sweater scraps, plaid wool scraps, home decor–weight fabric, in colors that will work nicely for your make-believe forest

Clean, empty vases or bottles

From the Crafter's Toolkit:

FriXion or fine-point pen

Straight pins

Ruler

Fabric scissors

Sewing machine and coordinating thread

TO MAKE:

1) **Create the tree templates and cut from the fabric.** Create rough templates by drawing a tall triangle on your fabric. Pin two layers of the fabric together and cut out two identical triangles to make one tree, adding ½ inch to the overall size for seam allowances. Experiment with the size. I wanted my trees quite narrow and thin, so I drew the triangles accordingly.

2) **Sew up the trees.** With right sides together, machine sew the two sides of the triangle, leaving the bottom open (no need to hem). Clip the bulk of the seam allowance from the top point and turn the triangle right side out.

3) **Display.** Fit the trees over empty vases or bottles in groups. If the trees are too tall, simply trim the excess off the bottom.

Fabric Scrap Flower Brooch

Using the exact same flower-making method we used for the Recycled Floral Mirror (page 35), a bunch of these scrap fabric flowers can make a pretty brooch or the "bow" for a gift.

MATERIALS:

Fabric flowers (see Recycled Floral Mirror, page 35)

Drinking glass

Piece of cardboard (perhaps from that shipping box you just put in the recycling bin?)

Pin backs (I used 1½-inch Darice nickel-plated)

From the Crafter's Toolkit:

Pencil

All-purpose scissors

Hot glue gun

TO MAKE:

1) **Create the flowers.** Make six to eight fabric flowers, following the instructions in the Recycled Floral Mirror project (page 35). Vary the color and the size to make an interesting bunch.

2) **Create the pin base.** Trace around the mouth of a drinking glass onto a piece of cardboard and cut out. Attach the flowers to the cardboard base, using hot glue, placing them very close together and hiding the cardboard completely.

   Hot glue the pin back to the center of the backside of the cardboard.

OTHER IDEA:

* Use these as tree ornaments, or string up bunches as a garland. In my studio, I have a large bunch of these flowers in a vase, made by adding a length of floral or craft wire to the back of the flower, then wrapping the wire with floral tape or strips of pretty fabric. It's a bouquet that never wilts!

Leather Appliquéd Pillow

You could easily substitute felt for the appliqué in this project, but the leather feels quite special. I look for leather clothing when thrift shopping; a jacket or skirt can be used for many projects. And don't let this project fool you into thinking its time consuming or complicated; you'll "appliqué" with glue, no hand stitching or thimbles needed!

MATERIALS:

¾ yard plaid or patterned fabric

2 colors of leather scraps (you will only need small amounts for this project, but if you are buying new leather, Tandy Leather is a great source)

1 (16-inch) square pillow form

Template for appliqué (page 178)

Scanner

Printer

A few sheets of card stock–weight paper

Digital camera (optional)

From the Crafter's Toolkit:

Iron and ironing board

Clear quilter's ruler

Rotary cutter and self-healing cutting mat

Paper scissors

FriXion or fine-point pen

Small sharp scissors

Fabric glue (I used Aleen's Super Fabric Adhesive)

Sewing machine and coordinating thread

Straight pins

Pinking shears (optional, for trimming raw edges)

TO MAKE:

1) **Cut the front and back pillow panel pieces.** Press the fabric. Cut one front panel piece measuring 16½ inches square, and two back panel pieces measuring 16½ x 10 inches. Set the two back panel pieces aside for now.

2) **Prepare the templates for the leather appliqué.** Make two copies of the Leather Appliqué pillow template (one for each color of leather). Carefully cut out the first template for color A. Using a FriXion or fine-point pen, trace the template onto the wrong side of the leather (remember to flip your template over to have it wrong side up, too). Repeat for color B.

3) **Cut out the leather.** As you cut out the pieces, using small sharp scissors, reassemble them on your work surface. (I found it helpful to take a digital photo of it all in place once everything was cut out.)

4) **Glue the appliqué onto the front pillow panel.** Fold the front pillow panel in half both lengthwise and widthwise, finger press to lightly mark the center of the panel. Place the appliqué pieces on the right side of the panel, working from the center of the pillow out. Once you have placed the appliqué as you like it, begin the gluing process by lifting up parts of the leather and painting a thin layer of glue on the underside, using a small paintbrush. Glue the small appliqué pieces onto the larger pieces first, then glue the larger pieces to the pillow panel, and then glue the surrounding pieces down. Allow it to dry flat overnight.

5) **Sew and finish the pillow.** First, machine hem the two back panel pieces. On one of the 16½-inch sides of each panel, fold ¼ inch to wrong side, press, then fold ¼ inch again to encase the raw edge, and press. Stitch this seam with coordinating thread, a ¼ inch away from the folded edge. Repeat with the other panel.

On your work surface, lay out the front cover, right side up, the top half of back cover, right side down, and bottom half of back cover, right side down (the hemmed edges of both panels should overlap at the middle of the pillow). Pin around all four sides and stitch, using a ¼-inch seam allowance. Trim around the edges with pinking shears, if desired. Trim bulk at corners, turn right side out, push the corners out, and press.

Insert the pillow.

Sewn Furniture

This is such a fun, unexpected way to adorn simple wooden furniture pieces. You could easily add tons of details, but why not present a family with their name in classic Helvetica font sewn right to the piece? Or adorn a wooden box with simple squares sewn in brightly colored yarn. There are lots of possibilities for a project like this and I leave it up to you to take it to the next level (as I know you can!).

MATERIALS:

Pieces of wooden furniture (e.g., tables or chairs)

Wood cleaner and cloth

Computer

Printer

All-purpose printer paper

Drill with a ⅛-inch drill bit

Yarn or string

From the Crafter's Toolkit:

Painter's blue tape

Pencil

Ruler

Size 9 crewel embroidery needle

TO MAKE:

1) **Clean the wooden piece thoroughly.** Once you decide what you will write, type it into the computer and adjust the size and layout until you are happy with it. I used a Helvetica font for the letters, but drew the squares on the box freehand. Enlarge the words to the desired size, print it out, and tape it to the piece with painter's blue tape. You will use it as a guide for drilling the holes.

2) **Drill the holes.** With a pencil, mark points about ¼ inch apart along the letters or shapes, and follow these to drill your holes. Drill the holes into the wood right through the paper template. Remove the template.

3) **Stitch the design.** Using yarn and the crewel needle, stitch the yarn through the holes, using a backstitch (this stitch is explained in step 3 of the Conversation Tablecloth project (page 32).

Knot off the threads on the underside of the piece.

Rain Boot Warmers

I wear rain boots quite often in the drippy, colder Seattle months. While they do a great job of keeping my feet dry, they aren't much on warmth. I thought about knitting a pair of boot warmers, but came up with a much quicker method, using a sweater that I no longer wear. I can't believe how much I love them.

MATERIALS:

One adult-size sweater

Paper

From the Crafter's Toolkit:

Measuring tape

Black fine-point marker

Paper and fabric scissors

Sewing machine and coordinating thread

Straight pins

TO MAKE:

1) **Make a template.** Measure the height of the rain boot from the ankle to the top. Add 3 inches to this measurement. Measure around the bottom, middle, and top parts of your calf to determine their circumference and add an inch to each measurement. Create a template by drawing these measurements on a piece of paper. Cut out the template.

2) **Cut the sweater pieces.** Cut open the sweater at both its side seams so you'll have two panels. Lay one panel on your work surface, right side down, and pin the paper template you made onto it, also right side down. If possible, orient the top of the boot warmer so that its cuff—the visible part sticking out over the top of the boot—will be the rib trim of the sweater. (Tip: If you are using a patterned sweater and want the pattern to show at the top of your boot, lay your template accordingly.) Trace around the template, then cut out. Repeat with the other panel.

3) **Sew the boot warmers.** Machine stitch along what will be the bottom edge of the boot warmer, with a zigzag or edge stitch, to finish it. If the top of the boot warmers are not a ribbed edge, you will need to do this around the top edge as well.

    With right sides together, pin each of the boot warmer pieces together along the long side seams. Machine stitch, using a ½-inch seam allowance. Turn right side out.

    Insert the warmers into your boot and fold a 2½-inch cuff over the top of the boot.

Advent Calendar

At least once every holiday season, my kids will ask me why they don't have a Lego-brand advent calendar. Oh, the sacrifices! But the tiny trinkets they find in the little pockets of this handmade version all but make up for it. Every year in late November, I pick an afternoon to grab a coffee and head out to shop for advent trinkets. It's a fun challenge to find things small enough to fit in the pockets, and I look forward to this every year. Take some time with this project, pick colors you love, and add some thoughtful details. You will pull it out every year, and it should always make you smile. Its finished size is 44 x 19 inches.

MATERIALS:

A wool camp blanket you can repurpose, or similar remnant that will give you a piece a roughly 46 x 19 inch-piece

Assorted colors of wool or craft felt for the pockets, pocket flaps, numbers, and trims in your chosen holiday color palette (I used red, cornflower blue, dark and light pea green, and a buttery yellow)

Lightweight cotton fabric scraps for the numbers and other embellishments (quilting and shirting weight cottons or anything that you can hand sew onto wool: I used a combination of solid and holiday printed quilting cottons for my numbers)

1 package double-sided fusible web (I used Pellon Wonder Under)

Computer (optional)

Printer (optional)

All-purpose printer paper (optional)

Embroidery floss in several colors (I used DMC)

Findings and trims (e.g., bells, cute buttons, charms, etc.), to embellish the pockets

Brown wool or felt scrap, for the roof and chimney

⅝-inch-diameter wooden dowel

Saw or heavy knife

1 yard ribbon

From the Crafter's Toolkit:

Quilter's clear ruler

Rotary cutter and self-healing cutting mat

Iron and ironing board

FriXion pen or water-soluble fabric marker

Fabric scissors

Hand-sewing needle

Straight pins

Fabric glue (I used Aleen's Super Fabric Adhesive)

TO MAKE:

1) **Prepare the blanket.** Using a quilter's clear ruler, rotary cutter, and cutting mat, cut the blanket to 46 x 19 inches. Set aside for now.

2) **Cut the advent pockets.** The pockets for Day 1 through Day 23 are cut 2½ x 3 inches. The pocket for Day 24 is cut 3½ x 3½ inches. Decide how many different colors of pockets you will have. (I had six red, six blue, three yellow, two light pea green, and seven dark pea green.) Cut twenty-three pocket flaps measuring 3¼ x 2 inches each and set aside for now.

3) **Create the numbers.** You will need numbers 1 through 24 for this project. Estimate how many numbers you'll cut from each fabric scrap, and iron a piece of double-sided fusible web to the back of each fabric, following the package instructions. (Tip: Keep in mind that you could also embroider some of the numbers directly onto the pockets, to add variety.) I drew my numbers freehand directly on the front of my fabric, using a FriXion pen, but you could also type them on a computer, print them out, and trace around them. Create and cut out all the numbers you'll need.

4) **Iron on and embroider the numbers to the pockets.** Appliqué the fabric numbers to the pockets by peeling the paper backing off the back and ironing onto the front of each pocket. If using DMC embroidery floss, separate the six strands of floss into two sets of three strands each; you will sew with three strands. Sew a running stitch around each of the numbers both to help them adhere to the pocket and to add more embellishment.

For any numbers you will embroider directly onto the pockets, simply write the number on the pocket, using a FriXion pen and embroider backstitches over the lines.

5) **Embellish the numbered pockets.** Add extra trims to the pockets, such as rickrack, ribbons, tiny charms, and so on, to further embellish them. (I sewed a few bells on ours to keep sneaky fingers away, and it truly works!)

6) **Create the roof.** Draw and cut out a simple triangular shape onto a scrap of brown wool, measuring 15 inches across and 7½ inches high. Next, draw and cut out a chimney rectangle measuring about 2½ x 2 inches. If you are adding an advent pocket to the roof, sew that and its pocket flap on before sewing the roof down. Sew the roof to the calendar base, using a running stitch and matching thread. The roof peak should be about 3¾ inches from the top edge of the calendar. Place the chimney on one side of the roof, cut off the bottom at an angle to meet the roofline, and hand stitch onto the calendar base, using a running stitch.

7) **Hand sew the advent pockets onto the calendar base.** Starting with the first row of pockets just below the roof, place four pockets about 1⅜ inches from the bottom edge of the roof, leaving about 3 inches between them. This does not have to be exact! Pin them in place, then sew them down to the calendar base on the sides and bottom, using contrasting thread and a running stitch. Sew the pocket flaps above each of them.

Evenly space the pockets for the next row, 1⅜ inches under the previous row, and repeat. Keep going in this manner to complete five rows, using the photo for guidance.

Sew on the bottom three pockets. The two pockets for the sixth row are positioned 1⅜ inches under the previous row, but each are centered under the two pockets above them, as shown in the photo. The bottom pocket, 24, is lowest, centered in the space between these two pockets.

8) **Create the outline of the house.** If you wish, once all the pockets are stitched on, embroider the outline of the house shape directly onto the calendar base with backstitches.

9) **Create the hanger.** Cut a wooden dowel to measure 19½ inches long. With the advent calendar laying right side down on a work surface, lay the dowel across the top edge. Add fabric glue across the top and roll the fabric completely around the dowel toward the back of the calendar. Cut a 30-inch length of ribbon. Tie each end of the ribbon in a firm knot on an end of the wooden dowel, adding a dot of glue to hold it in place. Allow to dry.

10) **Fill the advent calendar pockets!**

IDEAS FOR FILLING:

* Small erasers

* Unusual rocks

* Small chocolates

* Marbles

* Tiny plastic animals

* Charms (my kids like to think the tiniest ones are good luck)

* A message about a fun holiday activity (e.g., taking a drive to look at lights, special hot cocoa with sprinkles, a movie)

* Feathers

* Sample bottles of nail polish

* A tiny note written in invisible ink

* Riddles

* A set of jacks

Giant Cross-Stitched Tree

Stitching a giant tree is so much fun! Hardware store pegboard happens to be perfect for cross-stitch, and the resulting tree is just right for small spaces that can't fit a full-on holiday tree. I pulled every color of green yarn I had for my version, but it would be just as pretty (and the process would go much faster) using one skein of green yarn.

MATERIALS:

Sheet of pegboard measuring 48 x 32 inches (the holes on my sheet are spaced 1 inch apart)

White paint

1 skein green yarn or smaller amounts of several greens (I used 7 colors from my yarn stash)

Contrasting yarn for pompoms (I used 8 different colors)

Pompom maker kit (optional; I used Clover Pom Pom Makers)

From the Crafter's Toolkit:

Apron

Paintbrush

Pencil

All-purpose scissors

Ruler

Yarn needle

TO MAKE:

1) **Paint the pegboard.** Don your apron. Prepare the pegboard by giving it several coats of white paint (Tip: Don't worry if the holes pool with paint; simply poke your needle through later to open them up again.)

2) **Mark out the tree shape.** Hold the pegboard portrait-style so that it is 48 inches tall and 32 inches wide. Using a pencil, mark the first cross-stitch, which will start on the second row of holes from the top, in the very center. From there, following the photo, lightly mark all the spaces you will stitch. I put a tiny but visible X everywhere I would stitch, which was later covered by the yarn.

3) **Stitch your tree.** To stitch with several green shades as I did on mine, thread a long strand with one of the green yarns onto a yarn needle and make a few stitches here and there, then leave that strand hanging on the back of the board and switch to another green, and so on, picking up those strands and adding stitches here and there. If you use only one color of green, simply stitch from left to right, going from the top to the bottom of the tree. Knot each strand on the back when it's finished.

4) **Create the pompoms.** Make these in several sizes using your favorite method.

   To attach them to the tree, use a yarn needle and thread a 10-inch length of yarn through the center of the pompom, then thread both ends through a yarn needle. Insert the needle into a hole in the pegboard, pulling both tails through the board to the back, and secure the pompom to the board by tying a bow on the back of the board (this allows you to remove the pompoms later).

163

Handmade Checker Set

Inspired by the color and texture of an old woolen coat and paired with an obsession with wet felting rocks with wool roving I had one winter, I created a handmade set of checkers that continues to be used regularly at our house. Demonstrate to the small hands how to wet felt wool roving onto rocks and they will soon be more than happy to help. Search on Etsy.com for "wool roving supplies." If you don't want to use wool for the checkerboard base, other suitable fabrics are home decor–weight fabrics or canvas—any fabric that has a bit of body and weight. The finished size of the board is about 14 inches square; each of the checkers is about 1 inch across.

MATERIALS:

½ yard woven wool, for the base (the base of my set is dark charcoal gray)

¼ yard woven wool, for the contrasting squares (I used light gray)

½ yard heavyweight interfacing (I used Pellon Heavyweight Sew-in Interfacing)

Embroidery floss in contrasting colors (I used DMC)

24 flat river stones or pebbles, each measuring about 1 inch across (it's important for them to be flat, so they will stack)

Soap and water

At least 2 ounces each of 2 colors of pure wool roving

A pair of old stockings or pantyhose

Soap and a tub of hot water

Towel

From the Crafter's Toolkit:

Iron and ironing board

FriXion pen or water-soluble fabric marker

Quilter's clear ruler

Rotary cutter and self-healing cutting mat

Fabric scissors

Straight pins

Hand-sewing needle

Sewing machine and coordinating thread

TO MAKE THE CHECKERBOARD:

1) **Cut the fabric.** Press the wool. For the base of the checkerboard, cut two pieces from one color of your wool fabric, each measuring 15 inches square. Cut one square of heavyweight interfacing, also measuring 15 inches square.

   For the contrasting individual squares, cut thirty-two squares of the second color of wool fabric, each measuring 1¾ inches square.

2) **Create the checkerboard top.** On one piece of the base wool, lay out the thirty-two contrasting squares, four squares across by four squares down, alternating the placement of the squares on each row. Use a ruler to line up accurately and pin each in place. I found it easiest to line the squares up by starting from the middle of the "board" and working my way

outward. Leave ½ inch of space on all four sides of the base to allow for sewing your layers of the board together later.

If using DMC embroidery floss, separate the six strands of floss into two sets of three strands each; you will sew with three strands. Using a hand-sewing needle and contrasting embroidery thread, hand sew a running stitch around the perimeter of each square to secure it to the base. (There's no need to hem the edges of these squares.) Continue until all the squares are stitched down.

4) **Finish the checkerboard.** Lay out the layers on your work surface as follows: heavyweight interfacing panel; the back piece of 15-inch-square dark gray wool, wrong side down; and the front piece (with sewn squares), right side down. Pin the layers together around the perimeter.

Sew all the layers together. Beginning in the middle of one of the sides and using a ½-inch seam allowance, machine sew around all four sides, leaving a 4-inch opening on one of the sides for turning right side out. Backstitch to secure stitching.

Clip the corners to ease bulk, and turn the board right side out, gently pushing out the corners.

Lightly press the board. Fold the seam allowances at the opening in, finger press, and pin. Using matching thread, topstitch around the perimeter, through all layers, about ¼ inch from the edge, closing the open edge in the process.

The board is done!

5) **Prepare the rocks:** Clean the rocks with soap and water.

6) **Wet-felt the wool around the rocks.** (Important tip: Separate the wool roving by pulling apart the fibers, never by cutting.) Using one color of the wool roving and twelve of your stones, pull apart some of the wool fibers and begin wrapping around the first rock. This does not have to be a thick layer of wool, but for the wool to felt around the rock, the fibers must lay in a crosshatch pattern over it. After you've covered the rock with a layer of roving, put it into a stocking and tie it snugly closed.

Using warm to hot water and plenty of soap, immerse the rock in the water; rub it well on all sides with soapy water. Continue doing so for several minutes. The combination of the hot water, soap, and rubbing is what felts the wool. The wool will start to shrink, form, and felt around the rock. After about 5 minutes, try to untie the stocking to take a peek at your rock. If it's not yet felted, reclose and continue.

Do this process one or two more times, adding more wool roving each time and allowing the rocks to dry a bit between each cycle. By the end, the entire rock should be completely covered. As you complete each rock, place on a towel and allow to dry completely.

7) **Repeat with the second color of wool roving and second set of rocks.**

Knitted Swatch Blanket

These days, my kind of knitting is easy, knit stitches only (no purls), no counting, completely portable, and it eats through my yarn stash. I began knitting simple squares, which are really just a larger version of a typical knitter's gauge swatch (a sample piece, knitted with the yarn and recommended needles, to adjust for size and tension before moving on to the actual project), in an attempt to use up my seemingly endless supply of yarn. It was quick and something I could work on each night while I was watching a movie with my family (and it kept my hands out of the cookie jar). Once friends got wind of my easy evening knitting, they were sending their own knitted squares to me. So began the makings of my knitted swatch blanket. In addition to the hand-knit squares, I added squares of felted sweaters leftover from other projects to vary the texture, making this project finish up even quicker. This blanket has become a favorite at our house. Wrapping up under it reminds me of cozy evenings watching back-to-back seasons of Lost, of the knitted squares my friends contributed, and swatches of sweaters that belonged to loved ones. Gauge is not critical for this project, as long as all squares finish at the same size. The finished size of the blanket is about 45 inches square. Each of my squares finished at 8 inches across.

MATERIALS:

Good basic worsted-weight yarn (e.g., Cascade 220 100% wool yarn) in assorted colors (limit yourself to your own stash and you may create a surprisingly beautiful and unexpected color palette)

1 pair straight knitting needles compatible with your yarn (for mine, I used 4.5 mm [US size 7])

Felted wool sweaters in coordinating colors

1 color of coordinating yarn for sewing the squares together (I used charcoal gray)

From the Crafter's Toolkit:

All-purpose scissors

Ruler

Iron and ironing board

Straight pins

Yarn needle

A movie is a must. This type of knitting is best suited to multitasking.

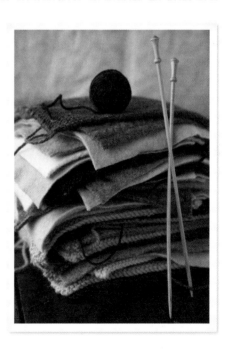

TO MAKE:

Cast on 45 stitches.

1) **Knit every row.** Continue until your swatch is square. It is not important that yours measure the same as mine, but all your squares need to be as close to the same size as you can get them. Continue knitting squares until you have the desired number.

2) **Cut squares from the felted sweaters.** Keep the size of these squares the same size as the knitted squares.

3) **Block the knitted squares.** Pin a knitted square directly to your ironing board's cover with straight pins, all around the perimeter, coaxing it into the finished size you want it to be (for mine, I pinned each square to 8 inches). Hold the iron directly above the square, not touching it, and let the steam penetrate the square for a several seconds. Allow the square to dry undisturbed. (Tip: I pinned as many squares as I could fit across my ironing board at one time, blocked them, then when they were nearly dry, took them up and did another batch, and so on, until I was done.)

4) **Lay out the blanket pattern.** Lay out both the knitted and the sweater squares in a pattern that you like, taking care to spread the color and texture all around the blanket. My blanket is six squares across and six squares down, so essentially a large square from the smaller squares.

5) **Sew the squares together.** Using a yarn needle with contrasting yarn, stitch the squares together, using about a ¼-inch seam allowance. I used a mattress stitch, which creates visible stitches only on the back of the blanket. To create this stitch, place two squares side by side on your work surface, right sides up. Leaving a long tail, and always working from back to front, insert the needle at the bottom right corner of the square on the left side. Next, inserting the needle from back to front, take a stitch on the bottom left corner of the right square. If you tug at both the long tail and the yarn end you are working with, the stitch will bring the two edges together, and neatly. Continue in this same manner all the way up the side of the square. To reinforce the edges, take a couple of extra stitches. Tie off the yarn securely on the back.

OTHER IDEAS:

✳ Add a flannel bedsheet to the back of this blanket, for a more substantial version.

✳ If you are an experienced knitter, try some more complicated stitches for added texture, maybe add a cable in the center of a square.

✳ Embroider some of the squares.

Avalon Quilt

I was online one evening, drooling over some amazing Dutch wallpaper, when my husband, Peter, called from Los Angeles where he was on business, saying, "You've got to see the wallpaper in this hotel." I couldn't believe it, but it was the exact same wallpaper I was looking at! My quilted version gives a nod to the triangular pattern of the original wallpaper, but with my own color combination. To make this quilt design effective, pick a palette of only three colors (which, in my example, is blue, green, and white) and use a variety of tonal and more contrasting shades within that color palette, which will make this quilt look deceivingly complex. I gathered and foraged a collection of well-loved yet outgrown corduroy pants and shirts both from our own closet and the thrift store to build my palette and make this quilt extra warm and textural. I will walk you through the nifty quilting trick of making the half-square triangles blocks that make up this entire quilt. The finished size is 47 x 55 inches. You can easily make this quilt larger or smaller by adding or subtracting rows of squares.

MATERIALS:

About 9 pairs of corduroy pants or shirts, skirts, or jackets in a variety of shades within your chosen palette of three main colors (I chose moss green, pea green, dark grayish blue, medium grayish blue, white, cream, medium blue, light blue, pale blue)

1 twin-size flat cotton flannel bedsheet in a coordinating color

1 package twin-size quilt batting (I used Warm & Natural 100% cotton batting)

½ yard 42- to 44-inch-wide cotton quilt-weight fabric, for binding (I used a light gray)

Walking foot for sewing machine (optional)

From the Crafter's Toolkit:

Fabric scissors

Iron and ironing board

Quilter's clear ruler

Quilter's clear square ruler measuring 4½ inches (optional, but helpful for squaring up your individual squares)

FriXion or fine-point pen

Sewing machine with coordinating thread

Rotary cutter and self-healing cutting mat

Painter's blue tape

Straight pins or binder clips

Quilter's or safety pins

Sewing machine needles for heavy-weight sewing (I used size 100/16)

Hand-sewing needle and coordinating thread

TO MAKE:

1) **Prepare the corduroy pieces.** Cut out all the usable areas (leg panels, etc.), so you can get as many squares as possible from each corduroy piece. (I did not use side seams, pocket areas, and so on, for this project, but you could.) Press well.

2) **Mark and cut out the squares.** As a general guide, plan to cut about fifteen 5-inch squares from each pair of pants. If you find you are a few short in one color, try cutting a few more in a similar color to compensate.

3) **Make the half-square triangles.** This quilt is constructed entirely of half-square triangles. To create two half-square triangles squares from two solid squares, begin by placing two contrasting fabric squares, right sides together, evenly on top of each other. Using a ruler and a fine-point pen, draw a diagonal line from one corner to the other. Machine stitch a line ¼ inch away from, and parallel to, the drawn line, on both sides of

it. Using a rotary cutter or fabric scissors, cut the squares apart directly on the drawn line, press the seams open, and voilà! You now have two squares of half-square triangles.

To make your quilt layout similar to mine, pair up your colored squares in the following groupings in the numbers specified, then combine them to make two-toned squares. You will start and end with 168 squares in total.

Blues and greens: 52 squares
Dark and light blues: 50 squares
White and blue: 48 squares
White and green: 16 squares
Whites: 2 squares

The squares will need to be squared up to 4½ inches (if you have a 4½-inch quilter's clear ruler it makes this step easier, but you can also use any clear quilter's ruler).

4) **Lay out the quilt top.** Begin laying out your pattern, row by row, following the illustration. A large floor or table area is helpful. To move this project to the sewing machine, stack each row from right (which will be the bottom of the stacked row) to left (top) in order, labeling each row by putting a piece of tape on the top square and labeling it "Row 1," "Row 2," and so on. Pin or clip each row together.

5) **Sew the quilt top together.** Do this one row at a time. With the first row at your machine, begin sewing the squares together, using a ¼-inch seam allowance, right sides together, and following the illustration to be sure the triangles are angled the correct way. (It's easy to get them turned around.) Sew the rows as you stacked them, from left to right. Press all the seams allowances open to distribute the bulk evenly throughout the quilt. Continue doing this row by row until each row is sewn together.

Next, sew the rows together, starting at the top row, right sides together. (Tip: Careful pinning on both sides of each seam will help them all match up.) Continue until the entire quilt top is pieced. Press the seams open.

6) **Make the quilt sandwich.** On a flat surface, lay out the backing layer (bedsheet), right side down. Use painter's blue tape to tape down and hold all four sides of this layer smoothly. Next, lay the quilt batting over that; and finished quilt top, right side up, on the top. Have at least 4 inches of quilt batting and backing extending beyond the quilt top on all four sides.

Baste the quilt layers together, working from the center front moving out. Pin the layers together, using quilter's or safety pins. Work outward in a grid pattern, placing pins every 6 inches or so. Once this step is completed, you can remove the tape and move the quilt, if needed. To move it, roll it up carefully.

7) **Quilt the layers.** To machine quilt, use machine needles specified for heavyweight fabrics or denim. For my quilt, I machine stitched ¼ inch away from the lengthwise seams of the quilt. This step requires some focus and patience, but don't be scared off by machine quilting. It is usually recommended to use a walking presser foot on your sewing machine if you have one, but know that I used an ordinary presser foot on the home machine I had at the time I made this quilt with great results. Starting in the center of the quilt, with the outer sides rolled toward the center area, sew a row of stitching ¼ inch away from seam line, on both sides of it. Remove the quilting pins and make sure all the layers are smooth as you go. Repeat for every seam going across the length of the quilt.

8) **Trim and square up the quilt.** Using a rotary cutter, quilter's clear ruler, and self-healing mat underneath, trim the edges of all the layers evenly to measure 47 x 55 inches.

9) **Create and sew on the binding.** Cut the binding fabric into six strips, selvedge to selvedge across the width of the fabric, each measuring 2½ inches wide. Sew the strips together end to end at a 90-degree angle, right sides together, until all of them are joined into one continuous strip. Fold and press the entire strip in half lengthwise, wrong sides together. Unfold one of the short edges of the binding, trim it at a 45-degree angle, fold ¼ inch of the cut edge to the wrong side, press, and refold. This will be the end you will begin at when sewing onto your quilt.

To attach the binding, start in the middle of one side of the quilt, and leave about 8 inches of the binding unsewn. With the raw edges of the binding aligned with the raw edge of the quilt, begin sewing the binding onto the front side, using a ⅜-inch seam allowance. Continue until you reach a corner. To create a mitered corner, stop ¼ inch from the edge and secure with a backstitch. Remove from under the presser foot. Next, fold the loose binding up and away from the quilt's edge at a 45-degree angle, but then fold it back down again, lining it up the raw edges with the edge of the quilt again. This creates the mitered fold. Turn the quilt 90 degrees and position the edge back under the machine, aligned to begin sewing the next side. Begin stitching ¼ inch from the fold you just made and continue along. Do this step for each corner.

Fold binding over the edge and hand stitch to the back of the quilt, using small hemstitches.

RESOURCES

Find me online at:

www.blairstocker.com

www.wisecrafthandmade.com

For leather supplies:

Tandy Leather, www.tandyleatherfactory.com

For beads and beading supplies:

Fusion Beads, www.fusionbeads.com

For general craft supplies:

Blick Art Materials, www.dickblick.com

Hobby Lobby, www.hobbylobby.com

Michaels, www.michaels.com

For fabric:

Drygoods Design, www.drygoodsdesignonline.com

Fabricworm, www.fabricworm.com

Joann's, www.joann.com

Pink Chalk Fabrics, www.pinkchalkfabrics.com

For secondhand goods and handmade items:

Etsy, www.etsy.com

Garage sales

Goodwill, www.goodwill.org

Locally owned thrift stores

Value Village/Savers, www.valuevillage.com

Blogs and websites to read for further inspiration:

3191 Miles Apart, www.3191milesapart.com

Alisa Burke, www.alisaburke.blogspot.com

Design Mom, www.designmom.com

Design Sponge, www.designsponge.com

Justina Blakeney, blog.justinablakeney.com

Little Green Notebook, www.littlegreennotebook.
  blogspot.com

Sania Pell at Home, www.saniapell.com

Young House Love, www.younghouselove.com

Books to inspire hand making for the home:

Domestic Bliss: How to Live by Rita Konig
  (Edbury Press, 2002)

Encyclopedia of Crafts (Random House, 2009) and
  Encyclopedia of Sewing and Fabric Crafts (Random
  House, 2010) by Martha Stewart

Handmade Living: A Fresh Take on Scandinavian Style
  by Lotta Jansdotter (Chronicle Books, 2010)

Made at Home: A Guide to Simple Sewing by Lisa Stickley
  (North Light Books, 2010)

Pure Style Living by Jane Cumberbatch (Dorling
  Kindersley, 2001)

TEMPLATES
Spooky Silhouettes

Leather Appliquéd Pillow

Color A (outlined areas)

Color B

*Note: Template should
be printed at 150%*

Hottie Rice Pillow

Note: Template should be printed at 130%

INDEX

Note: page references in *italics* indicate project photographs